THE
MISSIONARY
POSITION

05/17
17.00

Also by Christopher Hitchens

BOOKS

Hostage to History: Cyprus from the Ottomans to Kissinger
Blood, Class and Nostalgia: Anglo-American Ironies
Imperial Spoils: The Curious Case of the Elgin Marbles
Why Orwell Matters
No One Left to Lie To: The Triangulations of William Jefferson Clinton
Letters to a Young Contrarian
The Trial of Henry Kissinger
Thomas Jefferson: Author of America
Thomas Paine's "Rights of Man": A Biography
God Is Not Great: How Religion Poisons Everything
The Portable Atheist
Hitch-22: A Memoir
Arguably: Essays

PAMPHLETS

Karl Marx and the Paris Commune
The Monarchy: A Critique of Britain's Favorite Fetish
The Missionary Position: Mother Teresa in Theory and Practice
A Long Short War: The Postponed Liberation of Iraq

ESSAYS

Prepared for the Worst: Essays and Minority Reports
For the Sake of Argument
Unacknowledged Legislation: Writers in the Public Sphere
Love, Poverty and War: Journeys and Essays

COLLABORATIONS

James Callaghan: The Road to Number Ten (with Peter Kellner)
Blaming the Victims (edited with Edward Said)
When the Borders Bleed: The Struggle of the Kurds (photographs by Ed Kash)
International Territory: The United Nations (photographs by Adam Bartos)
Vanity Fair's Hollywood (with Graydon Carter and David Friend)

THE MISSIONARY POSITION

MOTHER TERESA IN THEORY
AND PRACTICE

Christopher Hitchens

SIGNAL
McCLELLAND
& STEWART

Signal is an imprint of McClelland & Stewart, a division of Random House Canada Limited

Published simultaneously in the United States of America by Twelve, an imprint of Grand Central Publishing.

Library and Archives Canada Cataloguing in Publication data available upon request

Typeset in Janson Text

Printed and bound in the United States of America

This book was produced using 20% recycled materials.

McClelland & Stewart,
a division of Random House of Canada Limited
One Toronto Street
Toronto, Ontario
M5C 2V6
www.mcclelland.com

1 2 3 4 5   16 15 14 13 12

For Edwin and Gertrude Blue:
saintly but secular.

Contents

Foreword

During the middle of the last decade, in his great period of political apostasy, Christopher Hitchens often entertained, along with his older left-leaning pals, a sprinkling of younger conservative journalists and operatives, all of them not only thrilled to be in his company—who ever wasn't?—but also grateful and deeply reassured to have such a blue-chip intellectual on their side of the Iraq War, that historical moment's great divide.

I would smile quietly while these young men cheered him on and *hear-hear*'d. Just wait, I'd think, knowing the moment would arrive when the ideological fiddler would have to be paid, when the host would change the topic and the earnest and happy young men would be reduced to looking at their shoes and muttering *Oh, well, yes, I suppose.* I like to think of this as the Mother Teresa Moment, named for Hitch's most incendiary cultural dissent but applicable to any subject that might startle the Christian soldiers of the Bush administration into remembering that, apart from Saddam Hussein, Hitch remained entirely his unreconstructed secular and socialist self.

Hitchens's disdain for the "thieving, fanatical Albanian dwarf"—i.e., Mother Teresa—became so famous that new readers of *The Missionary Position* may be surprised to discover that the phrase appears nowhere in this slender volume. If the book's main title produces a guffaw, its subhead ("Mother Teresa in Theory and Practice") more closely tracks its spirit. Far from being some cackle of defilement, or even just a bit of bad-boy blasphemy, *The Missionary Position* is, in fact, a modest, rational inquiry, a calm lifting of the veil that drapes its sacred subject. "Once the decision is taken to do without awe and reverence, if only for a moment," writes Hitchens, "the Mother Teresa phenomenon assumes the proportions of the ordinary and even the political." The author wishes to examine his subject's public pronouncements, her finances, projects and associates, and to judge "Mother Teresa's reputation by her actions and words rather than her actions and words by her reputation."

Does anyone have a problem with that?

What's under the veil turns out to be pretty unsightly: Mother Teresa's missions—backed by a yachtful of grifters from Haitian first lady Michèle Duvalier to 1980s S&L fleecer Charles Keating— are revealed to be less concerned with eliminating the poverty of the poor (and even their attendant physical pain) than with extending those things as their means toward salvation in the afterlife: "The point is not the honest relief of suffering but the promulgation of a cult based on death and suffering and subjection." Hitchens's most devastating source is "Mother" herself: She "has never pretended that her work is anything but a fundamentalist religious campaign," through which the poorest of the poor, the least of these, must grin and bear it until they're transmuted from being the last to the first.

Hitch being Hitch, he cannot, here and there, resist pouring it on for the reader's edified delight. Commenting upon the decision of advice columnist Ann Landers to share one of Mother's prescriptions for improving the world ("smile more"), he writes: "It is...doubtful whether a fortune-cookie maxim of such cretinous condescension would have been chosen even by Ann Landers unless it bore the imprimatur of Mother Teresa, one of the few untouchables in the mental universe of the mediocre and the credulous."

But *The Missionary Position* remains less a polemic than an investigation rooted in personal passion. In the manner of such intrepid, also-departed colleagues as Oriana Fallaci and Ryszard Kapuściński, Hitchens traveled the world toward eruptions of what fundamentally agitated him, and that was tyranny. "This is," he writes in the book's original foreword, "a small episode in an unending argument between those who *know* they are right and therefore claim the mandate of heaven, and those who suspect that the human race has nothing but the poor candle of reason by which to light its way." Preferring "antitheist" to "atheist," Hitchens liked to draw comparisons between Christianity and North Korea, both mental kingdoms offering their inhabitants the chance to commit "thought crime" and to deliver "everlasting praise" of the leader.

This small book is part of a big career devoted to pulverizing cant, deflating oppression, and maximizing human liberty. Not a day went by that Hitch didn't enter the lists against some iniquity. Nearly all his causes were noble; a few were quixotic and probably not worth his time. I remember one piece he wrote a half-dozen years ago in defense of free speech for David Irving, the Holocaust-denying historian. Writing against the clock, with his usual urgency, he made a slip of the keyboard in an attempted reference to one of Irving's editors, putting down "Thomas Mallon" for "Thomas Dunne." Oh, joy, I thought, seeing my name mistakenly next to Irving's in the pages of *The Wall Street Journal*. I sent Hitch an e-mail that began, more or less: "I know that to the sons of British naval officers all of us Micks must seem the same, but...." He responded late that night with "Oh, fuck," or words to that effect—no apology, just an injunction to turn up, the next day, at a demonstration he was organizing to support the Danish cartoonists who'd recently had the temerity to draw the prophet Mohammed. I thought about going, knew that I should, and finally never made it. If you want one more epitaph to add to all the ones that already have been suggested for this dual man-of-letters/man-of-action, let it be: He Showed Up. Throughout his life and times, whenever and wherever something important was on the line, he presented himself.

The Missionary Position appeared in 1995, eight years before Mother Teresa's beatification, an occurrence that Hitchens had seen rushing our way. He notes in his text how Pope John Paul II was readying so many candidates so quickly for this enhanced status ("the ante-room to sainthood") that the process had begun to "[recall] the baptism by firehose with which Chinese generals Christianized their armies."

In the event, Hitchens played a necessary, if negative, role in Mother Teresa's elevation, testifying before an official church body as to her unworthiness. He explained the task, undertaken in 2001, in the magazine *Free Inquiry*: "The present pope...has abolished the traditional office of 'Devil's Advocate,' so I drew the job of representing the Evil One, as it were, pro bono. Fine by me—I don't believe in Satan either." The writer's wife, Carol, can recall sending Hitch off to Father David O'Connor of the Washington, D.C., archdiocese to perform this strange and futile exercise in debunking, and then welcoming him home to lunch in their apartment on Columbia Road, as if he'd just come back from a radio interview.

Another, even more significant, development—this one, too, coming years after *The Missionary Position*—was the publication of Mother Teresa's letters. The spiritual doubts they were discovered to contain created a sensation worthy of the cover of *Time*. Let me present just one extract: "Jesus has a very special love for you," Mother Teresa wrote to the Reverend Michael Van Der Peet in 1979, the year she received her Nobel Peace Prize. "As for me, the silence and the emptiness is so great that I look and do not see, listen and do not hear." No, let's quote one more passage, just in case this was some momentary slip: "I am told God loves me—and yet the reality of darkness & coldness & emptiness is so great that nothing touches my soul."

You mean you're not sure?

Had these letters been available to him in the 1990s, I can hear Hitchens asking Mother Teresa just that question, face-to-face, as she showed him around the Calcutta orphanage. And it seems to me that the existence of such doubts makes her enterprise all the more breathtakingly presumptuous: She in fact was *not* one of "those who *know* they are right." She felt no certainty that the poverty she was barely palliating would lead its sufferers toward an eternal reward. It is one thing to take Pascal's wager and bet on the existence of God, no matter what one's doubts may be. But to lead thousands of others to the gaming table, insisting that they double down with their one paltry handful of chips?

After his cancer diagnosis, I often prayed, on my knees and through all my own doubts, for Hitch. Not for his soul; just for his earthly continuation. Nothing bothered me more during the long months of his illness (and suffering) than having to watch interviewers ask him if he might now not be ready to change his mind on matters cosmic. He met such inquiries with a sort of Christian forbearance, treated them as one more teachable moment in which he could explain his position. And throughout this grim period, by his conduct and example, he provided me with one specific religious certainty, the only one I've had in a very long time: If God does exist, He would have been deeply disappointed in any renunciation of nonbelief by Christopher Hitchens, that spectacular piece of His handicraft, the worthiest foe among all His brilliant, wayward sons of the morning.

Thomas Mallon
February 2012

One may safely affirm that all popular theology has a kind of appetite for absurdity and contradiction.... While their gloomy apprehensions make them ascribe to Him measures of conduct which in human creatures would be blamed, they must still affect to praise and admire that conduct in the object of their devotional addresses. Thus it may safely be affirmed that popular religions are really, in the conception of their more vulgar votaries, a species of daemonism.

David Hume, *The Natural History of Religion*

Nothing to fear in God. Nothing to feel in death. Good can be attained. Evil can be endured.

Diogenes of Oenoanda

Where questions of religion are concerned, people are guilty of every possible sort of dishonesty and intellectual misdemeanor.

Sigmund Freud, *The Future of an Illusion*

Acknowledgments

Who would be so base as to pick on a wizened, shriveled old lady, well stricken in years, who has consecrated her entire life to the needy and the destitute? On the other hand, who would be so incurious as to leave unexamined the influence and motives of a woman who once boasted of operating more than five hundred convents in upward of 105 countries—"without counting India"? Lone self-sacrificing zealot, or chair of a missionary multinational? The scale alters with the perspective, and the perspective alters with the scale.

Once the decision is taken to do without awe and reverence, if only for a moment, the Mother Teresa phenomenon assumes the proportions of the ordinary and even the political. It is part of the combat of ideas and the clash of interpretations, and can make no serious claims to having invisible means of support. The first step, as so often, is the crucial one. It still seems astonishing to me that nobody had ever before decided to look at the saint of Calcutta as if, possibly, the supernatural had nothing to do with it.

I was very much discouraged—as I asked the most obvious questions and initiated what were, at the outset, the most perfunctory investigations—by almost everybody to whom I spoke. So I must mention several people who gave me heart, and who answered the implied question—Is nothing sacred?—with a stoical "No." Victor Navasky, editor of *The Nation*, and Graydon Carter, editor of *Vanity Fair*, both allowed me to write early polemics against Mother Teresa even though they had every reason to expect a hostile reader response (which, interestingly, failed to materialize). In making the Channel Four documentary *Hell's Angel*, which aired in Britain in the autumn of 1994 and which *did* lead to venomous and irrational attacks, I owe everything to Vania Del Borgo and Tariq Ali of Bandung Productions, whose idea it was, and to Waldemar Januszczak of Channel Four, who "took the heat," as the saying goes. A secular Muslim, a secular Jew and a secular Polish Catholic made excellent company in fending off the likes of Ms. Victoria Gillick, a pestilential morals campaigner who stated publicly that our program was a Jewish/Muslim conspiracy against the One True Faith. Colin Robinson and Mike Davis of Verso were unwavering in their belief that a few words are worth many pictures. Ben Metcalf was and is a splendid copy editor.

This is a small episode in an unending argument

between those who *know* they are right and therefore claim the mandate of heaven, and those who suspect that the human race has nothing but the poor candle of reason by which to light its way. So I acknowledge as well the help and counsel and support of three heroes in this battle: Gore Vidal, Salman Rushdie and Israel Shahak. It was once well said, of the criticism of religion, that the critic should pluck the flowers from the chain, not in order that people should wear the chain without consolation but so that they might break the chain and cull the living flower. As fundamental monotheism and shallow cultism testify to one view of the human future, and as the millennium casts its shadow before us, it has been a privilege to soldier with such distinguished witnesses. If the baffled and fearful prehistory of our species ever comes to an end, and if we ever get off of our knees and cull those blooms, there will be no need for smoking altars and forbidding temples with which to honor the freethinking humanists, who scorned to use the fear of death to coerce and flatter the poor.

Ethiopians imagine their gods as black and snub-nosed; Thracians blue-eyed and red-haired. But if horses or lions had hands, or could draw and fashion works as men do, horses would draw the gods shaped like horses and lions like lions, making the gods resemble themselves.

Xenophanes

Introduction

On my table as I write is an old copy of *L'Assaut* ("The Attack"). It is, or more properly it was, a propaganda organ for the personal despotism of Jean-Claude Duvalier of Haiti. As the helplessly fat and jowly and stupid son of a very gaunt and ruthless and intelligent father (Jean-François "Papa Doc" Duvalier), the portly Dauphin was known to all, and to his evident embarrassment, as "Baby Doc." In an attempt to salvage some dignity and to establish an identity separate from that of the parental, *L'Assaut* carried the subtitle "*Organe de Jean-Claudisme.*"

But this avoidance of the more accurate "Duvalier-ism" served only to underline the banana-republic, cult-of-dynasty impression that it sought to dispel. Below the headline appears a laughable bird, which resembles a very plump and nearly flightless pigeon but is clearly intended as a dove, judging by the stylized sprig of olive clamped in its beak. Beneath the dismal avian is a large slogan in Latin—*In Hoc Signo Vinces* ("In this sign shall ye conquer")—which appears to negate the pacific and herbivorous intentions of the logo. Early Christian symbols, such as the cross or the fish, sometimes bore this superscription. I have seen it annexed on pamphlets bearing other runes and fetishes, such as the swastika. For a certainty, nobody could conquer anything under a banner bearing the device reproduced here.

On the inside, next to a long and adoring account of the wedding anniversary of Haiti's bulbous First Citizen and his celebrated bride, Michèle Duvalier, is a large photograph. It shows Michèle, poised and cool and elegant in her capacity as leader of Haiti's white and Creole elite. Her bangled arms are being held in a loving clasp by another woman, who is offering up a gaze filled with respect and deference. Next to the picture is a quotation from this other woman, who clearly feels that her sycophantic gestures are not enough and that words must be offered as well: *"Madame la Présidente, c'est une personne qui sent, qui sait, qui veut prouver son amour non seulement par des mots*, mais aussi par des actions concrètes et tangibles."[1] The neighboring Society page takes up the cry, with the headline: *"Mme la Présidente, le pays resonne de votre œuvre."*[2]

The eye rests on the picture. The woman proposing these lavish compliments is the woman known

---

[1] "Madame President is someone who feels, who knows, who wishes to demonstrate her love not only with words *but also with concrete and tangible actions*." [Emphasis added.]

[2] "Madame President, the country vibrates with your life work."

to millions as Mother Teresa of Calcutta. A number of questions obtrude themselves at once. First, is the picture by any chance a setup? Have the deft editors of *L'Assaut* made an exploited visitor out of an unsuspecting stranger, placed words in her mouth, put her in a vulnerable position? The answer appears to be in the negative, because the date of this issue is January 1981, and there exists film footage of Mother Teresa visiting Haiti that year. The footage, which was shown on the CBS documentary program *Sixty Minutes*, has Mother Teresa smiling into the camera and saying, of Michèle Duvalier, that while she had met kings and presidents aplenty in her time, she had "never seen the poor people being so familiar with their head of state as they were with her. It was a beautiful lesson for me." In return for these and other favors, Mother Teresa was awarded the Haitian *Légion d'honneur.* And her simple testimony, in warm encomium of the ruling couple, was shown on state-run television every night for at least a week. No protest against this footage is known to have been registered by Mother Teresa (who has ways of making her views widely available) between the time of the award and the time when the Haitian people became so "familiar" with Jean-Claude and Michèle that the couple had barely enough time to stuff their luggage with the National Treasury before fleeing forever to the French Riviera.

Other questions arise as well, all of them touching on matters of saintliness, modesty, humility and devotion to the poor. Apart from anything else, what was Mother Teresa doing in Port-au-Prince attending photo opportunities and award ceremonies with the local oligarchy? What, indeed, was she doing in Haiti at all? The world has a need to picture her in a pose of agonized yet willing subjection, washing the feet of Calcutta's poor. Politics is not her proper *métier*, and certainly not politics half a world away, in a sweltering Caribbean dictatorship. Haiti has been renowned for many years, and justly so, as the place where the wretched of the earth receive the cruelest and most capricious treatment. It is well and clearly understood, furthermore, that this is not the result of either natural disaster or unalterable misfortune. The island has been the property of an especially callous and greedy predatory class, which has employed pitiless force in order to keep the poor and the dispossessed in their place.

Let us look again at the photograph of the two smiling ladies. In terms of received ideas about Mother Teresa, it does not "fit." It does not, as people say nowadays, "compute." Image and perception are everything, and those who possess them have the ability to determine their own myth, to be taken at their own valuation. Actions and words are judged by reputations, and not the other way around. So hold the picture to the light for an instant, and try to take an impression of the "negative." Is it possible that the reverse black-and-white tells not a gray tale but a truer one?

Also before me as I write is a photograph of Mother Teresa standing, eyes modestly downcast, in friendly propinquity with a man known as "John-Roger." At first glance, it would seem to the casual viewer that they are standing in a Calcutta slum. A closer look makes it plain that the destitute figures in the background have been added in as a backdrop. The picture is a fake. So, for that matter, is John-Roger. As leader of the cult known sometimes as "Insight" but more accurately as MSIA (the "Movement of Spiritual Inner Awareness," pronounced "Messiah"), he is a fraud of Chaucerian proportions. Probably best known to the public for his lucrative connection to Arianna Stassinopoulos-Huffington—whose husband, Michael Huffington, spent $42 million of his own inherited money on an unsuccessful bid for a Senate seat in California—John-Roger has repeatedly claimed to be, and to have, a "spiritual consciousness" that is superior to that of Jesus Christ. Such a claim is hard to adjudicate. One might think, all the same, that it would be blasphemous to the simple outlook of Mother Teresa. Yet there she is, keeping him company and lending him the luster of her name and image. MSIA, it should be noted, has repeatedly been exposed in print as corrupt and fanatical, and the Cult Awareness Network lists the organization as "highly dangerous."

It turns out that the faked photograph records the momentous occasion of Mother Teresa's acceptance of a check for $10,000. It came in the form of an "Integrity Award" bestowed by John-Roger himself—a man who realized his own divinity in the aftermath of a visionary kidney operation. No doubt Mother Teresa's apologists will have their defense close at hand. Their heroine is too innocent to detect dishonesty in others. And $10,000 is $10,000 and, as Lenin was fond of saying (citing Juvenal), *pecunia non olet*: "money has no smell." So what is more natural than that she should quit Calcutta once more, journey to Tinseltown and share her aura with a guru claiming to outrank the Redeemer himself? We will discover Mother Teresa keeping company with several other frauds, crooks and exploiters as this little tale unfolds. At what point—her apologists might want to permit themselves this little tincture of skepticism—does such association cease to be coincidental?

One last set of photographs closes this portfolio. Behold Mother Teresa in prayerful attitude, flanked by Hillary Rodham Clinton and Marion Barry, as she opens an eight-bed adoption facility in the suburbs of Washington, D.C. It is a great day for Marion

Barry, who has led the capital city into beggary and corruption, and who covers his nakedness by calling for mandatory prayer in schools. It is a great day as well for Hillary Rodham Clinton, who almost single-handedly destroyed a coalition on national health care that had taken a quarter of a century to build and mature.

The seeds of this multiple photo opportunity, which occurred on 19 June 1995, were sown the preceding March, as the First Lady toured the Indian subcontinent. Molly Moore, the fine *Washington Post* reporter on the trip, made it clear in her dispatches that the visit was of a Potemkin nature:

> When the Clinton motorcade whisked through the Pakistani countryside yesterday, a long fence of brightly colored fabric shielded it from a sprawling, smoldering garbage dump where children combed through trash and several poor families had built huts from scraps of cardboard, rags and plastic. . . . In another instance, Pakistani officials, having heard rumors that the First Lady might take a hike into the scenic Margalla Hills overlooking the capital of Islamabad, rushed out and paved a 10-mile stretch of road to a village in the hills. She never took the hike (the Secret Service vetoed the proposal) but villagers got a paved road they'd been requesting for decades.

In such ways do Western leaders impress themselves momentarily upon the poor of the world, before flying home much purified and sobered by the experience. A stop at a Mother Teresa institution is absolutely *de rigueur* for all celebrities visiting the region, and Mrs. Clinton was not going to be the breaker of precedent. Having "raced past intersections where cars, buses, rickshaws and pedestrians were backed up as far as the eye could see," she arrived at Mother Teresa's New Delhi orphanage, where, again to quote from the reporter on the spot, "babies who normally wear nothing but thin cotton diapers that do little but promote rashes and exacerbate the reek of urine had been outfitted for the morning in American Pampers and newly-stitched floral pinafores."

One good turn deserves another, and so Mother Teresa's subsequent visit to Washington gave both Mrs. Clinton and Mayor Barry the occasion for some safe, free publicity. The new twelve-bed adoption center is in the rather leafy and decorous Chevy Chase suburb, and nobody was churlish enough to mention Mother Teresa's earlier trip to the city in October 1981, when she had turned the light of her countenance on the blighted ghetto of Anacostia. Situated in near segregation on the other side of the Potomac, Anacostia is the capital of black Washington, and there was suspicion at the time about the idea of a Missionaries of Charity operation there, because the inhabitants were known to resent the suggestion that they were helpless and abject Third Worlders. Indeed, just before her press conference, Mother Teresa found her office rudely invaded by a group of black men. Her assistant Kathy Sreedhar takes up the story:

> They were very upset.... They told Mother that Anacostia needed decent jobs, housing and services—not charity. Mother didn't argue with them; she just listened. Finally, one of them asked her what she was going to do here. Mother said: "First we must learn to love one another." They didn't know what to say to that.

Well, no. But possibly because they had heard it before. Anyway, when the press conference began, Mother Teresa was able to clear up any misunderstandings swiftly:

> "Mother Teresa, what do you hope to accomplish here?"
>   "The joy of loving and being loved."
>   "That takes a lot of money, doesn't it?"
>   "It takes a lot of sacrifice."
>   "Do you teach the poor to endure their lot?"
>   "I think it is very beautiful for the poor to accept

their lot, to share it with the passion of Christ. I think the world is being much helped by the suffering of the poor people."

Marion Barry graced the event with his presence, of course, as did Reverend George Stallings, the black pastor of St. Teresa's. Fourteen years later, Anacostia is an even worse slum and the Reverend Stallings has seceded from the Church in order to set up a blacks-only Catholicism devoted chiefly to himself. (He has also been in a spot of bother lately for allegedly outraging the innocence of a junior congregant.) Only Marion Barry, reborn in prison and re-elected as a demagogue, has really mastered the uses of redemption.

So behold again the photograph of Mother Teresa locked in a sisterly embrace with Michèle Duvalier, one of the modern world's most cynical, shallow and spoiled women: a whited sepulcher and a parasite on "the poor." The picture, and its context, announce Mother Teresa as what she is: a religious fundamentalist, a political operative, a primitive sermonizer and an accomplice of worldly, secular powers. Her mission has always been of this kind. The irony is that she has never been able to induce anybody to believe her. It is past time that she was duly honored, and taken at her word.

*   *   *

When I asked the electronic index at the Library of Congress to furnish me with a list of books on Mother Teresa, it printed out some twenty titles. There was *Mother Teresa: Helping the Poor*, by William Jay Jacobs; *Mother Teresa: The Glorious Years*, by Edward Le Jolly; *Mother Teresa: A Woman in Love*, which looked more promising but turned out to be by the same author in the same spirit; *Mother Teresa: Protector of the Sick*, by Linda Carlson Johnson; *Mother Teresa: Servant to the World's Suffering People*, by Susan Ullstein; *Mother Teresa: Friend of the Friendless*, by Carol Greene; and *Mother Teresa: Caring for All God's Children*, by Betsy Lee—to name but the most salient titles. Even the most neutral of these—*Mother Teresa: Her Life, Her Works*, by Dr. Lush Gjergji—proved to be a sort of devotional pamphlet in the guise of a biography, composed by one of Mother Teresa's Albanian co-religionists.

Indeed, the overall tone was so strongly devotional that it seemed almost normal for a moment. Yet if you review the above titles out loud—Mother Teresa, helper of the poor, protector of the sick, servant to the suffering, friend of the friendless—you are in fact mimicking an invocation of the Virgin and improvising your own "Ave Maria" or "Hail Mary." Note, too, the scale of the invocation—the *world's* suffering people, *all* God's children. What we have here is a saint in the making, whose sites and relics will one day be venerated and who is already the personal object of a following that is not much short of cultish.

The present Pope is unusually fond of the canonization process. In sixteen years he has created five times as many saints as all of his twentieth-century predecessors combined. He has also multiplied the number of beatifications, thus keeping the anteroom to sainthood well stocked. Between 1588 and 1988 the Vatican canonized 679 saints. In the reign of John Paul II alone (as of June 1995), there have been 271 canonizations and 631 beatifications. Several hundred cases are pending, including the petition to canonize Queen Isabella of Spain. So rapid and general is the approach that it recalls the baptism by firehose with which Chinese generals Christianized their armies; in one 1987 ceremony a grand total of 85 English, Scottish, Welsh and Irish martyrs were beatified in one day.

Sainthood is no small claim, because it brings with it the power to make intercession and it allows prayer to be directed at the said saint. Many popes have been slow to canonize, as the Church is generally slow to validate miracles and apparitions, because if divine intervention in human affairs is too promiscuously recognized, then an obvious danger arises. If one leper can be cured, the flock may inquire, then why not all lepers? Allow of a too-easy miracle and it becomes harder to answer questions about infant leukemia or mass poverty and injustice with unsatisfying formulae about the Lord's preference for moving in mysterious ways. This is an old problem, and it is unlikely to yield to mass-production methodology in the canonization division.

Although a "saint" traditionally is required to have performed at least one miracle, to have done "good works" and possessed "heroic virtues," and to have demonstrated the logistically difficult quality of ubiquity, many people who are not even Roman Catholics have already decided that Mother Teresa is a saint. Sources in the Vatican's "Congregation for Sainthood Causes" (which examines thorny cases like that of Queen Isabella) abandon their customary reticence and reserve in declaring Mother Teresa's beatification and eventual canonization to be certain. This consummation can hardly displease her, but it may not have been among her original objectives. Her life shows, rather, a determination to be the founder of a new order—her Missionaries of Charity organization currently numbers some 4,000 nuns and 40,000 lay workers—to be ranked with St. Francis and St. Benedict as the author of a "rule" and a "discipline."

Mother Teresa has a theory of poverty, which is also a theory of submission and gratitude. She has also a theory of power, which derives from St. Paul's neglected words about "the powers that be," which "are ordained of God." She is, finally, the emissary of a very determined and very politicized papacy. Her world travels are not the wanderings of a pilgrim but a campaign which accords with the requirements of power. Mother Teresa has a theory of morality too. It is not a difficult theory to comprehend, though it has its difficulties. And Mother Teresa understands very thoroughly the uses of the biblical passage concerning what is owed to Caesar.

As to what is owed to God, that is a matter for those who have faith, or for those who at any rate are relieved that others have it. The rich part of our world has a poor conscience, and it is no fault of an Albanian nun that so many otherwise contented people should decide to live vicariously through what they imagine to be her charity. What follows here is an argument not with a deceiver but with the deceived. If Mother Teresa is the adored object of many credulous and uncritical observers, then the blame is not hers, or hers alone. In the gradual manufacture of an illusion, the conjurer is only the instrument of the audience. He may even announce himself as a trickster and a clever prestidigitator and yet gull the crowd. *Populus vult decipi—ergo decipiatur.*

A Miracle

Convulsions in nature, disorders, prodigies, miracles, though the most opposite to the plan of a wise superintendent, impress mankind with the strongest sentiments of religion.

David Hume, *The Natural History of Religion*

Upon the whole, mystery, miracle and prophecy are appendages that belong to fabulous and not to true religion. They are the means by which so many Lo heres! and Lo theres! have been spread about the world, and religion been made into a trade. The success of one impostor gave encouragement to another, and the quieting salvo of doing some good by keeping up a pious fraud, protected them from remorse.

Tom Paine, *The Age of Reason*

Thus we call a belief an illusion when a wish-fulfillment is a prominent factor in its motivation, and in doing so we disregard its relations to reality just as the illusion itself sets no store by verification.

Sigmund Freud, *The Future of an Illusion*

Intercession, the hallmark of sainthood, requires the certification of a miracle. Mother Teresa is already worshipped as something more than human, but she has not transcended our common lot to the extent of being cited as a wonder-worker by Mother Church. The printout of the titles provided me by the Library of Congress showed that almost all were published in the 1980s and 1990s, and it wasn't until I had been through the list that I noticed what was not there: a 1971 book by Malcolm Muggeridge which argued, *inter alia*, that Mother Teresa's miracle had already taken place.

Muggeridge's book, *Something Beautiful for God*, was the outcome of a BBC documentary of the same name, screened in 1969. Muggeridge, who made something of a career out of ridiculing TV and showbiz values, claims that he began the project with no idea of the impression it would help to create. "Mother Teresa's way of looking at life is barren soil for copy-writers," he says, "and the poorest of the poor she cherishes offer little in the way of ratings." If that disingenuous disclaimer was true when filming began, it ceased to be true very shortly after transmission had occurred, for it is from this film and this book that we can date the arrival of Mother Teresa's "image" on the international retina.

Essential to Muggeridge's project, essential indeed to the whole Mother Teresa cult, is the impression that Calcutta is a hellhole:

> As it happened, I lived in Calcutta for eighteen months in the middle Thirties when I was working with the *Statesman* newspaper there, and found the place, even with all the comforts of a European's life—the refrigerator, the servants, the morning canter round the Maidan or out at the Jodhpur Club, and so on—barely tolerable.

Since Muggeridge's time, the city has not only had its own enormous difficulties to contend with but it has also been the scene of three major migrations of misery. Having been itself partitioned by a stupid British colonial decision before independence, Bengal took the brunt of the partitioning of all India into India and Pakistan in 1947. The Bangladesh war in 1971 and, later, the sectarian brushfires in Assam have swollen Calcutta's population to a number far greater than it can hope to accommodate. Photographs of people living on pavements have become internationally recognized emblems of destitution. Mother Teresa's emphasis on "the poorest of the poor and the lowest of the low" has served to reinforce the impression of Calcutta as a city of dreadful night, an impression which justly irritates many Bengalis.

The pleasant surprise that awaits the visitor to Calcutta is this: it is poor and crowded and dirty, in ways which are hard to exaggerate, *but it is anything but abject.* Its people are neither inert nor cringing. They work and they struggle, and as a general rule (especially as compared with ostensibly richer cities such as Bombay) they do not beg. This is the city of Tagore, of Ray and Bose and Mrinal Sen, and of a great flowering of culture and nationalism. There are films, theaters, university departments and magazines, all of a high quality. The photographs of Raghubir Singh are a testament to the vitality of the people, as well as to the beauty and variety of the architecture. Secular-leftist politics predominate, with a very strong internationalist temper: hardly unwelcome in a region so poisoned by brute religion.

When I paid my own visit to the city some years ago, I immediately felt rather cheated by the anti-Calcutta propaganda put out by the Muggeridges of the world. And when I made my way to the offices of the Missionaries of Charity on Bose Road, I received something of a shock. First was the inscription over the door, which read "He that loveth correction loveth knowledge." I don't know the provenance of the quotation, but it had something of the ring of the workhouse about it. Mother Teresa herself gave me a guided tour. I did not particularly care for the way that she took kisses bestowed on her sandaled feet as no more than her due, but I decided to suspend judgment on this—perhaps it was a local custom that I understood imperfectly. The orphanage, anyway, was moving and affecting. Very small (no shame in that) and very clean, it had an encouraging air and seemed to be run by charming and devoted people. One tiny cot stood empty, its occupant not having survived the night, and there was earnest discussion about a vacancy to be filled. I had begun to fumble for a contribution when Mother Teresa turned to me and said, with a gesture that seemed to take in the whole scene, "See, this is how we fight abortion and contraception."

If not for this, it would have been trifling to point out the drop-in-a-bucket contribution that such a small establishment makes to such a gigantic problem. But it is difficult to spend any time at all in Calcutta and conclude that what it most needs is a campaign against population control. Nor, of course, does

Mother Teresa make this judgment based on local conditions. She was opposed on principle to abortion and birth control long before she got there. For her, Calcutta is simply a front in a much larger war.

Muggeridge's fatalistic revulsion from the actual Calcutta made him all the more receptive to Mother Teresa's mystical prescription for the place, which is that it suffers from being too distant from Jesus. In consequence, his gullibility led him to write the following, which is worth quoting at length. (I should preface the quotation by saying that Muggeridge's BBC crew included a very distinguished camera-man named Ken Macmillan, who had earned a great reputation for his work on Lord Clark's art-history series *Civilisation*.)

This Home for the Dying is dimly lit by small windows high up in the walls, and Ken was adamant that filming was quite impossible there. We had only one small light with us, and to get the place adequately lighted in the time at our disposal was quite impossible. It was decided that, nonetheless, Ken should have a go, but by way of insurance he took, as well, some film in an outside courtyard where some of the inmates were sitting in the sun. In the processed film, the part taken inside was bathed in a particularly beautiful soft light, whereas the part taken outside was rather dim and confused....I myself am absolutely convinced that the technically unaccountable light is, in fact, the Kindly Light [Cardinal] Newman refers to in his well-known exquisite hymn.

Nor was Muggeridge attempting to speak metaphorically. Of the love he observed in the home, he wrote that it was

luminous, like the haloes artists have seen and made visible round the heads of the saints. I find it not at all surprising that the luminosity should register on a photographic film. The supernatural is only an infinite projection of the natural, as the furthest horizon is an image of eternity. Jesus put mud on a blind man's eyes and made him see.

Having gone on in this vein for some time, Muggeridge concluded:

This is precisely what miracles are for—to reveal the inner reality of God's outward creation. *I am personally persuaded that Ken recorded the first authentic photographic miracle.* [Emphasis added.]

Muggeridge did not exaggerate when he wrote "I fear I talked and wrote about it to the point of tedium." So it is interesting to have the direct testimony of Ken Macmillan himself:

During *Something Beautiful for God*, there was an episode where we were taken to a building that Mother Teresa called the House of the Dying. Peter Chafer, the director, said, "Ah well, it's very dark in here. Do you think we can get something?" And we had just taken delivery at the BBC of some new film made by Kodak, which we hadn't had time to test before we left, so I said to Peter, "Well, we may as well have a go." So we shot it. And when we got back several weeks later, a month or two later, we are sitting in the rushes theater at Ealing Studios and eventually up came the shots of the House of the Dying. And it was surprising. You could see every detail. And I said, "That's amazing. That's extraordinary." And I was going to go on to say, you know, three cheers for Kodak. I didn't get a chance to say that though, because Malcolm, sitting in the front row, spun round and said: "It's divine light! It's Mother Teresa. You'll find that it's divine light, old boy." And three or four days later I found I was being phoned by journalists from London news-papers who were saying things like: "We hear you've just come back from India with Malcolm Muggeridge and you were the witness of a miracle."

And a star was born. Ken Macmillan's testimony came far, far too late to prevent the spread, largely by the televisual and mass-media methods that

Muggeridge affected to despise, of the reported "miracle." Rather than "the first authentic photographic miracle," this episode is actually something considerably more significant. It is the first unarguable refutation of a claimed miracle to come not merely from another supposed witness to said miracle but from its actual real-time author. As such, it deserves to be more widely known than it is. But modern technology and communications have ensured instead that rumor and myth can be transmitted with ever greater speed and efficiency to the eyes and ears of the credulous. How splendidly we progress. Ever since *Something Beautiful for God*, the critic of Mother Teresa, in small things as well as in great ones, has had to operate against an enormous weight of received opinion, a weight made no easier to shift by the fact that it is made up, quite literally, of illusion.

Muggeridge gave numerous other hostages to fortune during the course of his film and his book. Only his adoring gaze, for example, inhibited him from seeing the range of interpretation that might be placed on the following anecdote:

As Simone Weil says, Christianity is a religion for slaves; we have to make ourselves slaves and beggars to follow Christ. Despite the chronic financial stringency of the Missionaries of Charity, when I was instrumental in steering a few hundred pounds in Mother Teresa's direction, she astonished, and I must say enchanted, me by expending it on the chalice and ciborium for her new novitiate....Her action might, I suppose, be criticized on the same lines as the waste of spikenard ointment, but it gave me a great feeling of contentment at the time and subsequently.

Of course if the purpose of Mother Teresa's work is that of strict religious proselytization and the founding of an order toward that end, there can be no conceivable objection to her employing charitable donations in order to decorate an altarpiece with the things of this world. But those who make the donations are, it seems, not always aware that this is the essential point. Mother Teresa, to her credit, has never claimed otherwise. She did not even bother to use the biblical story of the spikenard ointment in reassuring Muggeridge, telling him instead that "you will be daily on the altar close to the Body of Christ." Muggeridge was not then a Catholic, so he had no grounds on which to object that this was a doubly tricky use of the notion of transubstantiation. He thought of the spikenard alibi all by himself. (This is the passage in which Jesus breaks a costly box of unguent exclusively on his own feet. To the naive objection that the luxury item might with greater effect have been sold for the relief of poverty, he rejoins, "The poor you have always with you." I remember as a child finding this famous crack rather unsatisfactory. Either one eschews luxury and serves the poor or one does not. If the poor are always with us, on the other hand, then there is no particular hurry and they can always be used to illustrate morality tales. In which case, it might be more honest for their prophetic benefactors to admit that the poor have *us* always with *them*.)

Modesty and humility are popularly supposed to be saintly attributes, yet Mother Teresa can scarcely grant an audience without claiming a special and personal relationship with Jesus Christ. In the following exchange between Muggeridge and his star, who is the one demonstrating the self-abnegating modesty?

MUGGERIDGE: When I think of Calcutta and of the appallingness of so much of it, it seems extraordinary that one person could just walk out and decide to tackle this thing.

MOTHER TERESA: I was sure then, and I'm still convinced, that it is He and not I.

Here is a perfect fit between interviewer and subject: Muggeridge finds the poor of Calcutta to be rife with "appallingness," and Mother Teresa says that there would be no point in trying if one was not mandated by heaven. A little further on in the interview, Muggeridge inquires as follows:

> So you wouldn't agree with people who say there are too many children in India?

> MOTHER TERESA: I do not agree because God always provides. He provides for the flowers and the birds, for everything in the world that he has created. And those little children are his life. There can never be enough.

Muggeridge approves of this reply, saying moistly that Mother Teresa might as well be asked if there are too many stars in the sky. The entire dialogue is conducted in a semi-surreal manner, as if nobody had ever made any reasoned point about family planning or population policy. To say that there *are* too many children is to miss the point, because they are born already. But to say that there *cannot be* too many people is (and not only in India) to commit at least the sin of hubris. Mrs. Indira Gandhi—a political patron of Mother Teresa's, incidentally—once embarked upon a criminal campaign of forced sterilization in India. Clearly there are many ways of getting the population question wrong. On the other hand, there is no rational way of saying that the question does not arise. And if it were true that God "always provides," then, obviously, there would be no need for the Missionaries of Charity in the first place.

Before leaving Muggeridge's milestone behind us, it is necessary to record one more of the interchanges between him and his guru:

> MUGGERIDGE: You don't think that there's a danger that people might mistake the means for the end, and feel that serving their fellow men was an end in itself? Do you think there's danger of that?
>
> MOTHER TERESA: There is always the danger that we may become only social workers or just do the work for the sake of the work....It is a danger; if we forget to whom we are doing it. Our works are only an expression of our love for Christ. Our hearts need to be full of love for him, and since we have to express that love in action, naturally then the poorest of the poor are the means of expressing our love for God.

In the film of *Something Beautiful for God*, there is a sequence in which Mother Teresa takes an abandoned and undernourished child in her arms. The child is sickly looking and wizened and without much of the charm that babies possess at that age, but the old lady looks down at her with dauntless encouragement and enthusiasm and says, "See. There *is* life in her." It is an undeniably affirmative moment. We would not be worse off if there were many more like it. But, just as Mother Teresa rather spoiled her own best moment for me by implying that her life's work was a mere exercise in propaganda for the Vatican's population policy, she cheapens her own example by telling us, as above, that humanism and altruism are "dangers" to be sedulously avoided. Mother Teresa has never pretended that her work is anything but a fundamentalist religious campaign. And in the excerpt above we have it on her own authority that "the poorest of the poor" are the instruments of this; an occasion for piety.

Good Works
and
Heroic Virtues

Fan Ch'ih asked about wisdom. The master said: "To work for the things the common people have a right to, and to keep one's distance from the gods and spirits while showing them reverence can be called wisdom."

Confucius, *Analects Book VI, 22*

No Philosopher was on hand to tell him that there is no strong sentiment without some terror, as there is no real religion without a little fetishism.

Joseph Conrad, *Victory*

Star light, star bright . . . we look up and we hope the stars look down, we pray that there may be stars for us to follow, stars moving across the heavens and leading up to our destiny, but it's only our vanity. We look at the galaxy and fall in love, but the universe cares less about us than we do about it, and the stars stay in their courses however much we may wish upon them to do otherwise. It's true that if you watch the sky-wheel turn for a while you'll see a meteor fall, flame and die. That's not a star worth following; it's just an unlucky rock. Our fates are here on earth. There are no guiding stars.

Salman Rushdie, *The Moor's Last Sigh*

I

Those prepared to listen to criticism of Mother Teresa's questionable motives and patently confused sociological policy are still inclined to believe that her work is essentially humane. Surely, they reason, there is something morally impressive in a life consecrated to charity. If it were not for the testimony of those who have seen the shortcomings and contradictions of her work firsthand, it might be sufficient argument, on the grounds that Mother Teresa *must* have done some genuine good for the world's suffering people.

However, even here the record is somewhat murky and uneven, and it is qualified by the same limitations as apply to the rest of Mother Teresa's work: that such work is undertaken not for its own sake but to propagandize one highly subjective view of human nature and need, so that she may one day be counted as the beatific founder of a new order and discipline within the Church itself. Even in the quotidian details of ostensibly "charitable" labor, this unresolved contradiction repeatedly discloses itself.

Take, as one unremarked example, the visit of Dr. Robin Fox to the Mother Teresa operation in Calcutta in 1994. As editor of *The Lancet*, perhaps the world's leading medical journal, Dr. Fox was professionally interested in, and qualified to pronounce upon, the standards of care. The opening paragraphs of his report in the journal's 17 September 1994 issue also make it clear that he paid his visit with every expectation of being favorably impressed. Indeed, his tone of slightly raised-eyebrow politeness never deserts him:

> There are doctors who call in from time to time but usually the sisters and volunteers (some of whom have medical knowledge) make decisions as best they can. I saw a young man who had been admitted in poor shape with high fever, and the drugs prescribed had been tetracycline and paracetamol. Later a visiting doctor diagnosed probable malaria and substituted chloroquine. Could not someone have looked at a blood film? Investigations, I was told, are seldom permissible. How about simple algorithms that might help the sisters and volunteers distinguish the curable from the incurable? Again no. *Such systematic approaches are alien to the ethos of the home. Mother*

Teresa prefers providence to planning; her rules are designed to prevent any drift towards materialism: the sisters must remain on equal terms with the poor.... Finally, how competent are the sisters at managing pain? On a short visit, I could not judge the power of their spiritual approach, but I was disturbed to learn that the formulary includes no strong analgesics. Along with the neglect of diagnosis, the lack of good analgesia marks Mother Teresa's approach as clearly separate from the hospice movement. I know which I prefer. [Emphasis added.]

It should be underlined that the state of affairs described by Dr. Fox was not that obtaining in some amateur, impoverished clinic in a disaster zone. Mother Teresa has been working in Calcutta for four and a half decades, and for nearly three of them she has been favored with immense quantities of money and material. Her "Home for the Dying," which was the part of her dominion visited by Dr. Fox, is in no straitened condition. It is as he described it because that is how Mother Teresa wishes it to be. The neglect of what is commonly understood as proper medicine or care is not a superficial contradiction. It is the essence of the endeavor, the same essence that is evident in a cheerful sign which has been filmed on the wall of Mother Teresa's morgue. It reads "I am going to heaven today."

According to many other former volunteers, Dr. Fox may have paid his visit on an unusually good day, or may have been unusually well looked after. Mary Loudon, a volunteer in Calcutta who has since written extensively about the lives of nuns and religious women, has this testimony to offer about the Home for the Dying:

My initial impression was of all the photographs and footage I've ever seen of Belsen and places like that, because all the patients had shaved heads. No chairs anywhere, there were just these stretcher beds. They're like First World War stretcher beds. There's no garden, no yard even. No nothing. And I thought what is this? This is two rooms with fifty to sixty men in one, fifty to sixty women in another. They're dying. They're not being given a great deal of medical care. They're not being given painkillers really beyond aspirin and maybe if you're lucky some Brufen or something, for the sort of pain that goes with terminal cancer and the things they were dying of…

They didn't have enough drips. The needles they used and re-used over and over and over and you would see some of the nuns rinsing needles under the cold water tap. And I asked one of them why she was doing it and she said: "Well to clean it." And I said, "Yes, but why are you not sterilizing it; why are

you not boiling water and sterilizing your needles?"
She said: "There's no point. There's no time."

The first day I was there when I'd finished working in the women's ward I went and waited on the
edge of the men's ward for my boyfriend, who was
looking after a boy of fifteen who was dying, and an
American doctor told me that she had been trying
to treat this boy. And that he had a really relatively
simple kidney complaint that had simply got worse
and worse and worse because he hadn't had antibi-
otics. And he actually needed an operation. I don't
recall what the problem was, but she did tell me. And
she was so angry, but also very resigned which so
many people become in that situation. And she said,
"Well, they won't take him to hospital." And I said:
"Why? All you have to do is get a cab. Take him to
the nearest hospital, demand that he has treatment.
Get him an operation." She said: "They don't do it.
They won't do it. If they do it for one, they do it for
everybody." And I thought—but this kid is fifteen.

Bear in mind that Mother Teresa's global income
is more than enough to outfit several first-class clinics in Bengal. The decision not to do so, and indeed
to run instead a haphazard and cranky institution
which would expose itself to litigation and protest
were it run by any branch of the medical profession,
is a deliberate one. The point is not the honest relief

of suffering but the promulgation of a cult based on death and suffering and subjection. Mother Teresa (who herself, it should be noted, has checked into some of the finest and costliest clinics and hospitals in the West during her bouts with heart trouble and old age) once gave this game away in a filmed interview. She described a person who was in the last agonies of cancer and suffering unbearable pain. With a smile, Mother Teresa told the camera what she told this terminal patient: "You are suffering like Christ on the cross. So Jesus must be kissing you." Unconscious of the account to which this irony might be charged, she then told of the sufferer's reply: "Then please tell him to stop kissing me." There are many people in the direst need and pain who have had cause to wish, in their own extremity, that Mother Teresa was less free with her own metaphysical caresses and a little more attentive to actual suffering.

After I had helped to make *Hell's Angel*, a documentary about Mother Teresa's shortcomings which was screened on Channel Four in England in the autumn of 1994, I received a number of communications from former volunteers and even from former members of the Missionaries of Charity. Some wished to remain anonymous and some seemed actuated by motives of revenge or other personal disorders. My practice in citing the ones I consider to be genuine is as follows: the person must have been willing to be quoted by name and to give bona fide answers to some background questions. Let me instance Ms. Elgy Gillespie, author, journalist and sometime editor of *The San Francisco Review of Books*. Experienced in the care of AIDS patients, she spent some time at Mother Teresa's San Francisco branch:

Sent to cook in her hostel, tactfully named "The Gift of Love" (it is for homeless men with HIV), I found a dozen or so very sick men; but those who weren't very sick were exceptionally depressed, because they were not allowed to watch TV or smoke or drink or have friends over. Even when they are dying, close friends are not allowed. They are never allowed to drink, even (or especially) at the funerals of their friends and roommates and some have been thrown out for coming home in drag! When I mentioned the Olympics to them, they looked even more depressed. "We are not watching the Olympics," said a sister from Bombay, "because we are making our Lenten sacrifice." When they're very sick and very religious (which is often the case...) this doesn't matter, but with brighter men or older men it seems intolerable.

A Guatemalan writer that I befriended there was desperate to get out, so a friend of mine who also cooks there (an African American who is a practic-iñg Catholic) adopted him for as long as she could. He became much sicker and when she begged him to go back because she couldn't mind him, he begged her to keep him because he knew they didn't medi-cate enough, or properly, and was afraid he would have to die without morphine...I am now cooking occasionally for the homeless men at the Franciscans where one of the patients, Bruce, is an ex-Mother Teresa and neither he nor the priest have a good word to say for the Sisters at "The Gift of Love."

Many volunteers at hostels and clinics from Cal-cutta to San Francisco have comparable tales to relate. Especially impressive is the testimony of Susan Shields, who for nine and a half years worked as a member of Mother Teresa's order, living the daily discipline of a Missionary of Charity in the Bronx, in Rome and in San Francisco. I have her per-mission to quote from her unpublished manuscript, *In Mother's House*, which is an honest, well-written account, offered by a woman who left the Mission-aries of Charity for the same reason that she joined it—a love of her fellow humans.[3] If her memoir reads like the testimony of a former cult member, this is

---

[3] It seems to me a disgrace that such an original piece of courageous work should have failed to find a publisher when the Pope can receive an advance of around $5 million for a book he did not write.

because in many ways it is. She relates that, within the order, total obedience to the dictates of a single woman is enforced at every level. Questioning of authority is not an option.

I was able to keep my complaining conscience quiet because we had been taught that the Holy Spirit was guiding Mother. To doubt her was a sign that we were lacking in trust and, even worse, guilty of the sin of pride. I shelved my objections and hoped that one day I would understand the many things that seemed to be contradictions.

. . .

One summer the sisters in the Rome novitiate were given a great quantity of tomatoes. They couldn't give the tomatoes away because all their neighbors had grown their own. The superior decided that the sisters would can the tomatoes and eat them in the winter. When Mother came to visit and saw the canned tomatoes, she was very displeased. Missionaries of Charity do not store things but must rely only on God's providence.

. . .

In San Francisco the sisters were given use of a three-storey convent with many large rooms, long hallways, two staircases and an immense basement. . . . The sisters lost no time in disposing of the unwanted furnishing. They removed the benches from the chapel and pulled up all the carpeting in the rooms and hallways. They pushed thick mattresses out the windows and removed all the sofas, chairs and curtains from the premises. People from the neighborhood stood on the sidewalk and watched in amazement.

The beautifully constructed house was made to conform to a way of life intended to help the sisters become holy. Large sitting rooms were turned into dormitories where beds were crowded together.... The heat remained off all winter in this exceedingly damp house. Several sisters got TB during the time I lived there.

. . .

In the Bronx, plans were being made to establish a new home for the poor. Many of the homeless were sick and needed more permanent accommodation than that offered by our night shelter. We had bought a large abandoned building from the city for one dollar. A co-worker offered to be the contractor and arranged for an architect to draw up plans for the renovations. Government regulations required that an elevator be installed for the use of the disabled. Mother would not allow an elevator. The city offered to pay for the elevator. Its offer was refused. After all the negotiations and plans, the project for the poor was abandoned because an elevator for the handicapped was unacceptable.

This last anecdote may be familiar to some readers, because the New York press (which is fanatically loyal to Mother Teresa, as are most branches of the journalistic profession) wrote up the incident as a case of "politically correct" bureaucracy insisting on the rights of the disabled and negating the efforts of the missionaries. The truth is the exact reverse.

It might be argued that extreme simplicity, even primitivism, is to be preferred to a luxurious or corrupting style of the sort that has overtaken religious orders in the past. Ms. Shields told herself things like this for years. However, she realized that, rather than a life of ascetism, theirs was a regime of austerity, rigidity, harshness and confusion. As might be expected, when the requirements of dogma clash with the needs of the poor, it is the latter which give way.

She was disturbed that the poor were the ones who suffered from the sisters' self-righteous adherence to "poverty." She knew of immense quantities of money, donated in all sincerity by people "from all walks of life," which lingered unproductively in bank accounts, the size of which even many of the sisters knew nothing about. The sisters were rarely allowed to spend money on the poor they were trying to help. Instead they were forced to plead poverty, thus manipulating generous, credulous people and enterprises into giving more goods, services and cash. Ms. Shields became uncomfortable with the deceit, pretense and hypocrisy—the ancient problem of the Pharisees and the too-ostentatious public worshippers:

> The flood of donations was considered to be a sign of God's approval of Mother Teresa's congregation. We were told that we received more gifts than other religious congregations because God was pleased with Mother, and because the Missionaries of Charity were the sisters who were faithful to the true spirit of religious life. Our bank account was already the size of a great fortune and increased with every postal service delivery. Around $50 million had collected in one checking account in the Bronx.... Those of us who worked in the office regularly understood that we were not to speak about our work. The donations rolled in and were deposited in the bank, but they had no effect on our ascetic lives or on the lives of the poor we were trying to help.

Without an audit, it is impossible to say with certainty what becomes of Mother Teresa's hoards of money, but it *is* possible to say what the true purpose and nature of the order is, and to what end the donations are accepted in the first place. Susan Shields again:

For Mother, it was the spiritual well-being of the poor that mattered most. Material aid was a means of reaching their souls, of showing the poor that God loved them. In the homes for the dying, Mother taught the sisters how to secretly baptize those who were dying. Sisters were to ask each person in danger of death if he wanted a "ticket to heaven." An affirmative reply was to mean consent to baptism. The sister was then to pretend she was just cooling the person's forehead with a wet cloth, while in fact she was baptizing him, saying quietly the necessary words. Secrecy was important so that it would not come to be known that Mother Teresa's sisters were baptizing Hindus and Moslems.

Thus the smaller hypocrisy conceals a much greater one. "Our Constitution forbade us to beg for more than we needed, but the money in the bank was treated as if it did not exist." And thus the affectation of modesty and humility masks both greed and ambition, not to say arrogance.

I also have permission to quote from a letter I received from Emily Lewis, a seventy-five-year-old nurse who has worked in many of the most desperate quarters of the earth. At the time she wrote to me, she had just returned from a very arduous stint in Rwanda (a country about which Mother Teresa has been silent, perhaps because the Roman Catholic leadership in that country was complicit in the attempted genocide of the Tutsi people in the summer of 1994). Ms. Lewis's testimony follows:

My own experience of Mother Teresa occurred when she was being honored at the 1989 luncheon meeting of the International Health Organization in Washington, D.C. During her acceptance speech, she spoke at length of her opposition to contraception and her activities to save the unwanted products of heterosexual activity. (She also touched on AIDS, saying she did not want to label it a scourge of God but that it did seem like a just retribution for improper sexual conduct.) Although she said that God could find it in his heart to forgive all sinners, she herself would never allow a woman or a couple who had had an abortion to adopt one of "her" babies. In her speech Mother Teresa frequently referred to what God wants us to think or do. As my table-mate (an MD from Aid to International Development) remarked to me: "Do you think it takes a certain amount of arrogance to assume that you have a direct line to God's mind?"

Is it going too far to liken Mother Teresa to some of our infamous televangelists, turning their audiences on to what is in God's heart and mind while encouraging and accepting all donations?

The rich world likes and wishes to believe that someone, somewhere, is doing something for the Third World. For this reason, it does not inquire too closely into the motives or practices of anyone who fulfills, however vicariously, this mandate. The great white hope meets the great black hole; the mission to the heathen blends with the comforting myth of Florence Nightingale. As ever, the true address of the missionary is to the self-satisfaction of the sponsor and the donor, and not to the needs of the downtrodden. Helpless infants, abandoned derelicts, lepers and the terminally ill are the raw material for demonstrations of compassion. They are in no position to complain, and their passivity and abjection is considered a sterling trait. It is time to recognize that the world's leading exponent of this false consolation is herself a demagogue, an obscurantist and a servant of earthly powers.

II

The Catholic Church is a limitless source of fascination, to believers as well as to doubters and unbelievers, because of its attitude toward sex and procreation. Its official dogmas, derived in the main from St. Paul but elaborated down the centuries, forbid clergy from being married and prohibit women from being clergy. Homosexual acts are condemned, as in a way are homosexual persons. Heterosexual acts taking place outside the bond of lawful matrimony are condemned, whether premarital or extramarital. The sexual act within marriage is frowned upon unless it has reproduction as its object. Solitary sex is taboo. The preaching of such a range of prohibitions, and its enforcement by male and female celibates, has been the fertile soil for innumerable reflections, autobiographies and polemics from the *Confessions* of St. Augustine to Mary McCarthy's *Memoirs of a Catholic Girlhood*.

Reverence for life, especially in its vulnerable condition *in utero*, is a *sine qua non* of Catholic teaching, and one which possesses a great moral strength even in its extreme forms. A woman experiencing danger in childbirth, for example, is supposed to sacrifice her own life for that of the child. (Judaism, which has codes no less ethical, tends to mandate the opposite decision, for the greater good of the family.) When mass rapes occurred in the course of aggressive war in Bangladesh and later in Bosnia, Mother Teresa in the first case and the Pope in the second made strenuous appeals to the victims not to abort the seed of the invader and the violator. Give the child up for adoption, or raise it in a spirit unlike the one in which it was conceived—this was the injunction. While it can be seen as grotesque to lecture women who are in such desperate dilemmas, there is none the less something impressive and noble in the high priority the Church gives to potential life. Humans, it says, blaspheme when they throw away a fetus, because they cannot assume the right to dispose of another's life and they cannot presume to know the future. Children born with appalling deformities in sordid and overcrowded homes have been known time and again, after all, to defy all material odds and become exemplary, or merely human.

But the nobility of this essential teaching is compromised by the fact that it depends on an unnecessary theological assumption about "ensoulment"—the

point at which Thomas Aquinas maintained that a
life became human and immortal. Two objections
can be made here, the first being that human life can
and should be respected whether or not it is consti-
tuted by a creator with an immortal soul; to make
the one position dependent upon the other is to
make the respect in some way contingent. Second, if
a fertilized egg is fully human, then all terminations
of pregnancy at any stage and for any reason are to
be regarded as murder. This offends against the natural or instinctive feeling in favor of the pregnant
woman and the occupant of her womb, because it
blurs the distinction between an embryonic group
of cells and a human with a central nervous system.
The distinction between abortions in the first and
third trimesters, a distinction which speaks both to
our ability to avoid casuistry and to our inborn wish
to have a say in our own fates, is therefore null and
void in Catholic teaching. Some of the coarsening in
arguments on the other side of the case—arguments
which bluntly and unscientifically define the fetus
as a mere appendix to the woman's body—no doubt
result from confrontation with this absolutist edict.

Then there is the fact that Catholic prohibition on
abortion comes indissolubly linked to a prohibition
on birth control and contraception. Again, more is
involved than the technical and dogmatic finding

that certain forms of contraception, such as some versions of the intrauterine device which expels fertilized ova, actually are abortifacient in the fundamentalist definition of the term: the ban extends to all means and methods of avoiding conception, and indeed to the very intention of doing so. It is as "natural" in humans to seek control over their biological fecundity as it is for them to wish to have children in the first place. The Roman Catholic Church stands alone in condemning the desire to remove oneself from the caprices of nature and evolution, and the Roman Catholic Church has great political power over millions of poor and fertile people.

The Church's teaching seems to deny any connection at all between the rapid exponential growth in human population and the spread and persistence of disease, famine, squalor, ignorance and environmental calamity. One need not be a follower of the grim Reverend Malthus to deduce that there is indeed such a connection and that, moreover, it works in the other direction as well. In every developing country that has been studied, a clear correlation can be found between the limitation of family size and the life chances of the family members. Where such measures cannot be freely taken, by means of education and example, they have been enforced in desperation by authoritarian regimes. We have before us the forbidding example of the People's Republic of China, which limits families to one child apiece and is thus, in the name of Communism, preparing a future in which the words "brother" and "sister" will have no literal meaning. And we have the instance of Mother Teresa's friend and admirer Indira Gandhi, who launched a demagogic and brutal attempt to bring about male sterilization by a combination of bullying and bribery. (Salman Rushdie's short story "The Free Radio" in *East, West* brilliantly shows the pathos and emptiness of this effort.) Certainly these are not kind solutions, but they evidence the severity of a problem which the Church has chosen entirely to ignore.

Over the past decades, and particularly since the Second Vatican Council, the Roman Catholic Church has been faced with nearly every sort of cultural, doctrinal and political dissent. In Latin America, where it faces an unprecedented challenge from evangelical Protestantism and from the populist challenge of so-called "liberation theology," the need to renew the priesthood has led to questioning of the celibacy requirement. In the United States and Western Europe, the congregation appears to conduct its affairs without reference to canonical teaching on birth control. Homosexual groups have petitioned for the right to be considered true Catholics, since if God did not create their condition there seems to be an interesting question as to who did. Even prominent Catholic writers of the conservative wing, such as William Buckley and Clare Booth Luce, have made the obvious point that an unyielding opposition to contraception, and the ranking of it as a sin more or less equivalent to abortion, is, among other things, a cheapening of the moral position on abortion itself.

In all of these debates, the most consistently reactionary figure has been Mother Teresa. The fundamentalist faction within the Vatican has found her useful in two ways—first as an advertisement for the good works of the Church to non-Catholics; and second as a potent instrument of moral suasion within the ranks of the existing faithful. She has missed no opportunity to restate elementary dogmas (much as she once told an interviewer that, if faced with a choice between Galileo and the authority of the Inquisition, she would have sided with the Church authorities). She has inveighed against abortion, against contraception and against the idea that there should be any limit whatsoever to the growth of world population.[4]

---

[4] In the course of preparing for the 1994 United Nations World Population Conference in Cairo, the Vatican went so far as to make a temporary alliance with those forces of Shi'a Islam, chiefly represented by the mullahs of Iran, which denounced population control as an imperialist conspiracy. The apple of dogma had, at least in this case, fallen some distance from the tree of proselytization and the crusades.

*   *   *

When Mother Teresa was awarded the Nobel Peace Prize in 1979, few people had the poor taste to ask what she had ever done, or even *claimed* to do, for the cause of peace. Her address to the ceremony of investiture did little to resolve any doubt on this score and much to increase it. She began the speech with a literal-minded account of the myth of Christ's conception, perhaps in honor of that day's festal character: the Feast of the Immaculate Conception. Then she began her diatribe:

> I was amazed when I learned that in the West so many young people are on drugs. I tried to understand the reason for this. Why? The answer is, "because in the family there is nobody who cares about them." Fathers and mothers are so busy they have no time. Young parents work, and the child lives in the street and goes his own way. We speak of peace. These are the things that threaten peace. I think that today peace is threatened by abortion, too, which is a true war, the direct killing of a child by its own mother. In the Bible we read that God clearly said: "Even though a mother did forget her infant, I will not forget him."
>
> Today, abortion is the worst evil, and the greatest enemy of peace. We who are here today were wanted by our parents. We would not be here if our parents had not wanted us.

We want children, and we love them. But what about the other millions? Many are concerned about the children, like those in Africa, who die in great numbers either from hunger or for other reasons. But millions of children die intentionally, by the will of their mothers. Because if a mother can kill her own child, what will prevent us from killing ourselves, or one another? Nothing.

There is not much necessity for identifying the fallacies and distortions which are piled upon one another here. Few women who have had abortions, even those who still feel remorse or regret, will recognize themselves as having committed actual infanticide. If there are "millions" of children being slain in this way, so that they compare to the millions of children dying of malnutrition and pestilence, then there is clearly no hope for Mother Teresa's adoption solution. (She claims to have rescued only three or four dozen orphans from the entire Bangladesh calamity, for example.) Moreover, these impressive figures should be enough at least to impel reconsideration in those who proclaim that all pregnancies are "wanted" by definition and that there can be no excess population.

At a vast open-air mass in Knock, Ireland, in 1992, Mother Teresa made it plain yet again that there is no connection at all in her mind between the conditions of poverty and misery that she "combats" and the inability of the very poor to reach the plateau on which limitation of family size becomes a rational choice. Addressing a crowd of the devout, she said, "Let us promise Our Lady who loves Ireland so much that we will never allow in this country a single abortion. And no contraceptives."

In this instance, she fell into the last great fallacy and offense to which Church teaching on this subject is prone. Ireland is now, to a great extent, a secular society. It is also a society which has to seek an accommodation with its huge Protestant-majority province. The Church claims the right to make law, in states where it is strong enough, for believers and unbelievers alike. Mother Teresa's "pacific" humanitarianism and charity therefore translate directly into an injunction to the faithful to breed without hindrance, an admonishment to the rest to live under laws not made by them, and an attack on the idea of a non-sectarian state. What this does for the cause of peace does not, in Ireland, take long to estimate. What it does for suffering humanity is to criminalize, or at least to ration and restrict, one of the few means ever devised for its self-emancipation. It is often said, inside the Church and out of it, that there is something grotesque about lectures on the sexual life when delivered by those who have shunned it. Given the way that the Church forbids women to preach, this point is usually made about men. But given how much this Church allows the fanatical Mother Teresa to preach, it might be added that the call to go forth and multiply, and to take no thought for the morrow, sounds grotesque when uttered by an elderly virgin whose chief claim to reverence is that she ministers to the inevitable losers in this very lottery.

III

In her reputation-making interview with Malcolm Muggeridge during *Something Beautiful for God*, Mother Teresa made the following large claim:

> We have to do God's will in everything. We also take a special vow which other congregations don't take; that of giving wholehearted free service to the poor. This vow means that we cannot work for the rich; neither can we accept any money for the work we do. Ours has to be a free service, and to the poor.

For the many ethical humanists, as well as for the many vaguely religious people who support or endorse what they imagine to be Mother Teresa's mission, the above statement is quite an important one. It seems to spare the Missionaries of Charity from the worldliness and financial cunning which have so disfigured Christianity in the past. And it insists that no service is furnished to the rich—a claim which might lead the unwary to conclude that no contributions are solicited from them.

In point of fact, the Missionaries of Charity have for decades been the recipients of the extraordinary largesse of governments, large foundations, corporations and private citizens. The affectation of poverty, which is so attractive to some observers, has obscured this relative plenty. And so has another affectation—one very well known to missionary fund-raisers down through the years. In this story, which has become solemnized by repetition at a thousand tent meetings, the necessary donation arrives just at the moment when the need for it is greatest. Was a consignment of blankets the pressing need, with a hard winter coming on? Sure enough, an anonymous benefactor chose that very night to leave a truckload of blankets on the doorstep of the mission. Dr. Lush Gjergji gives an especially touching example of the genre in his book, an example no less touching for its being written as if the notion had never been tried out in print before:

One day Sister Frances, from the city of Agra, phoned Mother Teresa asking for urgent help.

"Mother, I need 50,000 rupees. Over here there is a crying and urgent need to start a house for the children."

Mother Teresa replied: "That is too much, my daughter, I will call you back; for the moment we have nothing…" A short time later the phone rang again. It was a press agency. "Mother Teresa? This is the editor of the agency. The Philippine government has just awarded you the Magsaysay Prize. Heartfelt compliments! It involves a considerable sum."

Mother Teresa: "Thanks for letting me know."

The editor: "What do you plan on doing with the 50,000 rupees from the prize?"

Mother Teresa: "What did you say? 50,000 rupees? I think the Lord wants us to build a home for children at Agra."

As her television reputation spread, Mother Teresa found herself accepting more and more awards and benefactions. The Indian government invested her with the Prize of the Miraculous Lotus. In 1971 the Vatican gave her the John XXIII Prize for Peace (Dr. Gjergji hastens to inform us that on this occasion "the prize winner herself had come to the Vatican on the city bus, and was wearing her Indian sari, worth about one dollar." If true, this was ostentatious of her.) In Boston in the same year she accepted the "Good Samaritan" award, again with many words of self-deprecation. Then straight to Washington, to receive the John F. Kennedy award on 16 October. The next year, with the auction in full swing, the government of India improved on its relatively lowly Miraculous Lotus prize and gave her a larger one, in a ceremony at which Indira Gandhi publicly wept. In 1973 it was Prince Philip's turn to make an emotional demonstration, which he did while presenting the Templeton Prize "for the promotion of faith in the world." In the presence of his wife, who holds the title of "Defender of the Faith" against all the works of Rome and who heads a family which is barred from making a marriage to a Roman Catholic, the royal consort handed over £34,000. The United Nations Food and Agriculture Organization went one better two years later by striking a special medal with the goddess Ceres brandishing a stalk of wheat at Mother Teresa and, on the obverse, the inscription "Food For All: Holy Year 1975." Revenue from the sale of the medals went to the Missionaries of Charity. It was only a step up from this to the Albert Schweitzer Prize, and then to yet another recognition from the Indian government—this time an honorary degree presented by Indira Gandhi herself. (The future patroness of compulsory sterilization had become, in the meantime, head of the government.) In March 1979, the International Balzan Prize, worth a quarter of a million lire, was presented by the president of Italy. The Pope, by then John Paul II, took the opportunity of her visit to receive her in private audience. All things thereby pressed toward the ultimate event of the prize-giving machine, which was to make Mother Teresa the Nobel Laureate for Peace and to invest her with the prize and the check in December 1979.

Nobody has troubled to total the amount of prize money received from governments and quasi-government organizations by the Missionaries of Charity, and nobody has ever asked what became of the funds. It is safe to say, however, that if all the money had been used on one project it would have been possible, say, to give Calcutta the finest teaching hospital in the entire Third World. That such is neither Mother Teresa's intention nor her desire may be inferred from the Muggeridge incident. It may also be inferred from her preference for spreading the money thin and for devoting it to religious and missionary work rather than the sustained relief of deprivation. In any event, if she is claiming that the order does not solicit money from the rich and powerful, or accept it from them, this is easily shown to be false.

The apologists generally claim that Mother Teresa is too innocent to count money or to take the measure of those who offer it, or to reckon that they obtain some benefit from their supposed generosity in the form of virtue-by-association. Forgetting for a moment her boast that she does not accept eye-of-the-needle subventions in the first place, we might agree that this argument had merit in the case of the late Robert Maxwell. Mr. Maxwell inveigled a not-unwilling Mother Teresa into a fund-raising scheme run by his newspaper group, and then, it seems (having got her to join him in some remarkable publicity photographs), he made off with the money. But Maxwell did succeed in fooling some very experienced and unsentimental people in his day, and although it might be asked how Mother Teresa had time to spare for such a wicked and greedy man, it can still be argued with some degree of plausibility that she was a blameless party to his cynical manipulations.

However, it is difficult, if not impossible, to assert this in the case of Mr. Charles Keating. Keating is now serving a ten-year sentence for his part in the Savings and Loan scandal—undoubtedly one of the greatest frauds in American history. In the early 1980s, during the booming, deregulated years of Reagan's first term, Keating, among other operators, mounted a sustained and criminal assault on the deposits of America's small investors. His methods were those of the false prospectus and the political bribe. (Washington vernacular still contains the expression "the Keating Five," in honor of the five United States senators who did him favors while receiving vast campaign donations in the form of other people's money.) Keating had political ambitions as well as financial ones, and as a conservative Catholic fundamentalist had served Richard Nixon as a member of a much-mocked commission to investigate the ill effects of pornography.

At the height of his success as a thief, Keating made donations (not out of his own pocket, of course) to Mother Teresa in the sum of one and a quarter million dollars. He also granted her the use of his private jet. In return, Mother Teresa allowed Keating to make use of her prestige on several important occasions and gave him a personalized crucifix which he took everywhere with him.

In 1992, after a series of political and financial crises and the most expensive bailout operation in the history of the American taxpayer, Keating was finally brought to trial. He appeared before the Superior Court in Los Angeles (his "Lincoln Savings and Loan" had been a largely Californian operation) where he was heard by the later-notorious Judge Lance Ito. The trial could have only one outcome: the maximum sentence allowable under California law.

During the course of the trial, Mother Teresa wrote to the court seeking clemency for Mr. Keating. She gave no explanation of her original involvement with the defendant and offered no direct testimony mitigating his looting of the thrift industry. The letter, in its original form, appears opposite.

One is struck immediately by two things. First, though the claim about "free service to the poorest

"As long as you did it to one of these My least brethren. You did it to Me"

FILED

JAN 27 1992

HANK S ... COUNTY CLERK

C. Liebe

DEPUTY

18/1/92

Honorable Lance Ito
Superior Court
210 West Temple Street
Dept. 123, 13th floor
Los Angeles, Calif. 90012

Dear Honorable Lance Ito,

We do not mix up in Business or Politicts or courts. Our work, as Missionaries of Charity is to give wholehearted and free service to the poorest of the poor.

I do not know anything about Mr. Charles Keating's work or his business or the matters you are dealing with.

I only know that he has alway been kind and generous to God's poor, and always ready to help whenever there was a need. It is for this reason that I do not want to forget him now while he and his family are suffering. Jesus has told us "Whatever you do to the least of my brethern...YOU DID IT TO ME. Mr. Keating has done much to help the poor, which is why I am writing to you on his behalf.

Whenever someone asks me to speak to a judge, I always tell them the same thing. I ask them to pray, to look into thier heart, and to do what Jesus would do in that circumstance. And this is what I am asking of you, your Honor.

My gratitude to you is my prayer for you, and your work, your family and the people with whom you are working.

God bless you
M. Teresa mc

of the poor" is made in almost the same words as it was made to Muggeridge, the related claim that the rich receive no quid pro quo seems to have disappeared. Then there is the astonishing artlessness of the letter, both as composed and as presented. One might think it a missive from an innocent old woman who knows nothing of cupidity and scandal, and who naively wishes to intercede for reasons of rather woolly compassion. The transcript of Mother Teresa's highly ideological Nobel Prize speech, for example, does *not* read like this. It is professionally written and presented. And many of her other public interventions demonstrate a much sharper sense of the real world, even when Mother Teresa is choosing to speak on matters, such as sexuality and reproduction, where she must necessarily admit to being disqualified by inexperience.

The suspicion that there might be something *faux naïf* about the appeal occurred also to Mr. Paul Turley who, in his capacity as Deputy District Attorney for Los Angeles, was Mr. Keating's co-prosecutor. On his own initiative, and as a private citizen, he wrote and dispatched a careful reply. I reproduce it below for the first time:

Dear Mother Teresa:
    I am a Deputy District Attorney in Los Angeles County and one of the persons who worked

on the prosecution of your benefactor, Charles H. Keating, Jr. I read your letter to Judge Ito, written on behalf of Mr. Keating, which includes your admission that you know nothing about Mr. Keating's business or the criminal charges presented to Judge Ito. I am writing to you to provide a brief explanation of the crimes of which Mr. Keating has been convicted, to give you an understanding of the source of the money that Mr. Keating gave to you, and to suggest that you perform the moral and ethical act of returning the money to its rightful owners.

Mr. Keating was convicted of defrauding 17 individuals of more than $900,000. These 17 persons were representative of 17,000 individuals from whom Mr. Keating stole $252,000,000. Mr. Keating's specific acts of fraud were that he was the source of a series of fraudulent representations made to persons who bought bonds from his company and he also was the repository of crucial information which he chose to withhold from bond purchasers, thereby luring his victims into believing they were making a safe, low-risk investment. In truth and in fact, their money was being used to fund Mr. Keating's exorbitant and extravagant lifestyle.

The victims of Mr. Keating's fraud come from a wide spectrum of society. Some were wealthy and well-educated. Most were people of modest means and unfamiliar with high finance. One was, indeed, a poor carpenter who did not speak English and had his life savings stolen by Mr. Keating's fraud.

The biblical slogan of your organization is "As long as you did it to one of these My least brethren. You did it to Me." The "least" of the brethren are among those whom Mr. Keating fleeced without flinching. As you well know, divine forgiveness is available to all, but forgiveness must be preceded by admission of sin. Not only has Mr. Keating failed to admit his sins and his crimes, he persists in self-righteously blaming others for his own misdeeds. Your experience is, admirably, with the poor. My experience has been with the "con" man and the perpetrator of the fraud. It is not uncommon for "con" men to be generous with family, friends and charities. Perhaps they believe that their generosity will purchase love, respect or forgiveness. However, the time when the purchase of "indulgences" was an acceptable method of seeking forgiveness died with the Reformation. No church, no charity, no organization should allow itself to be used as salve for the conscience of the criminal. We all are grateful that forgiveness is available but we all, also, must perform our duty.

That includes the Judge and the Jury. I remind myself of the biblical admonition of the Prophet Micah: "O man, what is good and what does the Lord require of you. To do justice, love mercy and walk humbly."

We are urged to love mercy but we must *do* justice.

You urge Judge Ito to look into his heart—as he sentences Charles Keating—and do what Jesus would do. I submit the same challenge to you. Ask yourself what Jesus would do if he were given the fruits of a crime; what Jesus would do if he were in possession of money that had been stolen; what Jesus would do if he were being exploited by a thief to ease his conscience?

I submit that Jesus would promptly and unhesitatingly return the stolen property to its rightful owners. You should do the same. You have been given money by Mr. Keating that he has been convicted of stealing by fraud. Do not permit him the "indulgence" he desires. Do not keep the money. Return it to those who worked for it and earned it!

If you contact me I will put you in direct contact with the rightful owners of the property now in your possession.

Sincerely,
Paul W. Turley

Three years later, Mr. Turley has received no reply to his letter. Nor can anybody account for the missing money: saints, it seems, are immune to audit.

This is by no means the only example of Mother Teresa's surreptitious attitude to money, nor of her hypocritical protestations about the beauty of poverty, whether self-imposed or otherwise. But it is the clearest and best-documented instance, and it is proof against the customary apologetics about innocence and unworldliness. In her dealings with pelf, as in her transactions with power, Mother Teresa reigns in a kingdom that is very much of this world.

Ubiquity

Naturally, there are puzzles. I would like to know whether or not the universe is finite or infinite. I would like even better to be assured that the two words are meaningless. But excepting the sort of puzzle which makes our passage here interesting and gives incentive to our questioning games, I see no mystery at the heart of things and take comfort from Wittgenstein's profoundly unpopular dictum, "Philosophy simply puts everything before us, and neither explains nor deduces anything. Since everything lies open to view there is nothing to explain. For what is hidden, for example, is of no interest to us."

Gore Vidal, *Two Sisters*

The Bible commands us to love our enemies. I love the Pope very much.

Father Jean-Bertrand Aristide,
president of Haiti

I

At a certain point in the period of its medieval ascendancy, the Church of Rome was forced to confront a problem of theory and of practice. If a human soul could only be redeemed by acceptance of the New Testament canon—the birth, life, death and resurrection of Jesus Christ—then what was to become of those who had never heard the news? These were not heretics or infidels to be slain or burned but people who suffered from "invincible ignorance." They fell into two categories: those who lived in parts of the world unvisited and untouched by the faith, and those who had died before the Christian era began. (There was also a third category, namely the disciples of Jesus himself, who had never read the Bible story, either. But they were, and remain, exempt.) Not much could be done for those who had expired before the birth of Christ, though Dante did his best for them and there are passages in the Creeds which speak of Jesus descending into hell in order to carry out some retrospective redemption. But for those who lived in non-Christian lands, it was decreed that the work of conversion was an imperative.

It is, in a sense, a pity that this work will always be remembered for its association either with conquest, with religious fratricide or with imperialism. Very frequently, the main consequence was sanguinary conflict between different branches of Christianity itself. (Long after the Catholic Crusaders got to Jerusalem, for example, they sacked Orthodox and Byzantine Constantinople.) In later epochs, both Catholic and Protestant missionaries penetrated the interiors of China and Japan and the remotest parts of Africa and South America, but their presence was indissoluble from that of the trading post and the garrison. In the course of a profitable partnership with slavery, colonialism and forced labor, the Christian "civilizing mission" often came up against strongly entrenched local religions. Where it did not adapt to these, or eliminate their believers, it made little headway. In India, which was disputed as a prize between four principal European powers before passing under British suzerainty, the effect of Christianity has been relatively slight. The Indian authorities, who are suspicious to this day of the link between proselytization and foreign interference, have generally dis-

couraged missionary activity. They have left Mother
Teresa's Missionaries of Charity largely alone, however, in deference to the worldwide reputation of
their founder. The Mother Teresa establishment in
Calcutta, therefore, possesses elements of pathos and
nostalgia: it is the chief and lonely relic of what was
once a vast enterprise of conquest and crusading.

When the girl Agnes Bojaxhiu was born on 27
August 1910 in Skopje, to an Albanian Catholic
family, the idea of the "mission" as a vocation was
still very much alive. And in that region, yesterday
as today, allegiance to the Church was more than
a merely confessional matter. It was, and is, imbri-
cated with a series of loyalties to nation, region and
even party. We know little enough of Agnes's early
life, and the devotional tracts written about her are
not very illuminating, but it seems that her father
Nikola, a prosperous shopkeeper, died in a nationalist squabble when the girl was only eight. The family
was strongly religious and adhered to the Parish of
the Sacred Heart, which in Skopje was synonymous
with Albanian identity. Through the influence of
a Jesuit priest she became interested in missionary
work and at the age of twelve, on her own account,
she first received the idea that her life should be ded-
icated to spreading the word among the poor. But
she told Malcolm Muggeridge that "at the begin-
ning, between twelve and eighteen, I didn't want to

become a nun. We were a very happy family. But when I was eighteen, I decided to leave my home and become a nun." Having entered a convent—the Congregation of the Sisters of the Blessed Virgin Mary of Loreto—she left Skopje for Zagreb, and from there traveled to Dublin, where the Loreto Sisters have their headquarters to this day. Shortly after Christmas Day 1928, her ship made landfall in Colombo, en route to the Loreto mission in Bengal.

The account of Agnes's early life given by Dr. Gjergji is intriguing for its fragmentary character. We learn, for example, that the future Mother Teresa's brother, Lazzaro, "went to Italy in 1939, remained there during and after the war, and finally died there." We learn also that "when, in the fall of 1910, the Serbians reached Skopje, the missionaries had to limit their pastoral action to the city itself. Things got worse at the outbreak of war in 1914." From this terse account we can only guess at the impact on the fervent Bojaxhiu family of the second Balkan war and the two world wars. However, a certain amount of background can be inferred.

Albanians divide between members of the Tosk and Gheg peoples, separated south and north, respectively, by the Shkumbini river. Most are Muslim, with an Orthodox Christian minority among the Tosks and a Roman Catholic one among the Ghegs. The Ghegs, who include the Bojaxhiu family, populate the much-disputed region of Kosovo. Now an "autonomous region" of Serbia, Kosovo has an Albanian majority, but it is also home to the Orthodox Serbs' holiest battlefield—the site of a fourteenth-century rout by the Turks.

In 1927 King Zog of Albania signed a treaty with Benito Mussolini which made Albania into an effective protectorate of Italian fascism. The treaty provided for the training of the Albanian military by Italian officers and the relocation of the Bank of Albania to Rome. Even before the subsequent Concordat signed between Mussolini and the Vatican, which gave papal imprimatur to the fascist project, the treaty established favorable conditions for the adoption of Roman Catholicism throughout Albania. The Church was permitted to open numerous schools, while the schools run by Greek Orthodox authorities were closed. (Greece took Albania to the World Court on this matter and in 1933 won a landmark case defining the rights of minorities to their own language and religion.) Nor did the advent of the Second World War diminish the enthusiasm of "Greater Albania" for the Axis. Even as Hitler was taking over Athens, a delegation of Albanian notables waited upon Mussolini in order to present him with the crown of Skanderbeg, the Albanian national hero.

A striking fact about this period is the fealty of all Albanian extremists to the idea of "Mother Albania."

When Mussolini finally collapsed, the Albanian Communists, under the leadership of Enver Hoxha, echoed, at a meeting of Albanian political groups that included the fascists, the demand that Kosovo be incorporated into Albania after the war. Tito's partisans were strong enough and (then) weighty enough in Moscow to negate this demand. But many of Hoxha's postwar cabinet members were unpurged members of the Albanian Youth of the Lictor, a prewar fascist movement which cherished the idea of military expansion. (Hoxha's successor as dictator, Ramiz Alia, was one of those who made this bizarre yet seemingly consistent traverse of the political spectrum.)

Before the war, the ideas of fascism, Catholicism, Albanianism and Albano-Italian unity were closely identified. Afterward, religious identity was officially suppressed by Hoxha's proclamation of the "world's first atheist state." None the less, the evidence implies that irredentist ideology persisted under Stalinist disguise and had at least as much to do with Albania's foreign-policy alignments as did any supposed doctrinal schism over the canonical texts of Marx and Lenin. An Albanian Catholic nationalist, in other words, might, on "patriotic" questions, still feel loyal to an ostensibly materialist Communist regime.

How else are we to explain the following entry from the *Yearbook on International Communist Affairs 1990*, published by the Hoover Institution at Stanford University and reviewing developments in all countries of the Communist world?

> After numerous previous attempts to secure a visa had been denied, in August the government allowed Mother Teresa to visit Tirana....Although the visit was called "private," Mother Teresa was received by Mrs. Hoxha, Foreign Minister Reis Malile, Minister of Health Ahmet Kamberi, the Chairman of the People's Assembly Petro Dode, and other state and party officials. Dutifully, the Albanian-born nun and Nobel peace prize laureate placed a wreath at the monument of "Mother Albania" and "paid homage and laid a bouquet of flowers on the grave of Comrade Enver Hoxha." The world-renowned Catholic nun did not utter a word of criticism against the regime for its brutal suppression of religion.

The "Mother Albania" monument, it might be worth emphasizing, is not an abstract symbol of sentimental nationhood. It is the emblem of the cause of Greater Albania. A nearby museum displays the boundaries of this ambition in the form of a map. "Mother Albania" turns out to comprise—in addition to the martyred province of Kosovo—a large piece of Serbia and Montenegro, a substantial chunk of formerly Yugoslav Macedonia and most of that part of modern Greece now known as Epirus.

I possess a film of "Mother Teresa" making her homage to "Mother Albania"—as well as to its patron, the pitiless thug Enver Hoxha—and it invites the same question as does the infamous embrace in Haiti: What is a woman of unworldly innocence and charity doing *dans cette galère?* Apologists have said, of the Albanian case, that it was only natural for Mother Teresa to make a few obeisances in order to visit the graves of her ancestors and, of the second, that a few compromises were necessary so that her order would be allowed to work freely in Haiti. Interestingly enough, these are not excuses that have been tendered by Mother Teresa herself, who keeps her own counsel on both matters (and on many others besides).

It is at least worth considering whether Mother Teresa made both of these trips (and many others) in furtherance of the more flinty political stands taken by hard-liners in her own Church. The personal conduct and the questionable policy are at least congruent in each instance. In the case of Haiti, the Vatican had long taken a position in favor of the "Duvalierist" oligarchy. When the Reverend Father Jean-Bertrand Aristide began his campaign of charismatic populism against the regime, he encountered instant hostility from the Church hierarchy, which eventually suspended him from his order. By the time that Aristide had been triumphantly elected, ignominiously deposed by a military junta and finally restored to power by international intervention, the Vatican was the only government in the world which still retained formal diplomatic relations with the usurping dictatorship. Mother Teresa's activism, then, was representative of the most dogmatic line taken by her Church.

Similarly in the Balkans, the collapse and disintegration of Yugoslavia led to a recrudescence of essentially prewar rivalries. Croatia, with the support of the Vatican and Germany, declared itself an independent state and restored many of the signs and emblems of the wartime republic led by Ante Pavelic. Protected by the Vatican and the Third Reich, this government had massacred its Jews and embarked on a program of forced conversion of Orthodox Serbs; those who resisted the crusade had been put to death. This memory alone, and the evident lack of regret for it, contributed to the evolution of a nationalist-religious paranoia among the Serbs, who subsequently launched a war of territorial and sectarian aggrandizement, destroying the cities of Vukovar and Sarajevo in the process. The Croatian ruling party, led by Franjo Tudjman, responded by carving out its own slice of Bosnia and demolishing the city of Mostar.

Even more ominously there existed, and still exists, the possibility that a generalized war could destroy the boundaries of the former Yugoslavia and once again pit Catholic against Orthodox as well as both, in various local combinations, against Islam. In Tetovo, the Albanian center of western Macedonia, and in Kosovo too, local zealots speak of Greater Albania as the response to Greater Serbia, and they flourish their pictures of Mother Teresa.

II

Intervention, whether moral or political, is always and everywhere a matter of the most exquisite timing. The choice of time and the selection of place can be most eloquent. So indeed may be the moments when nothing is said or done. Mother Teresa is fond of claiming to be not so much *above* politics as actually *beyond* them, operating in a manner that is transcendental. All claims by public persons to be apolitical deserve critical scrutiny, and all claims made by those who affect a merely "spiritual" influence deserve a doubly critical scrutiny. The naive and simple are seldom as naive and simple as they seem, and this suspicion is reinforced by those who proclaim their own naïveté and simplicity. There is no conceit equal to false modesty, and there is no politics like antipolitics, just as there is no worldliness to compare with ostentatious antimaterialism.

Mother Teresa's timing shows every sign of

instinctive genius. She possesses an intuition about the need for her message and about the way in which this message should be delivered. To take a relatively small example: In 1984 the Indian town of Bhopal was the scene of an appalling industrial calamity. The Union Carbide plant, which had been located in the town to take advantage of low labor costs and government tax incentives, exploded and spilled toxic chemicals over a large swath of the citizenry. Two and a half thousand persons perished almost at once, and many thousands more were choked by lung-searing emissions and had their health permanently impaired. The subsequent investigation revealed a pattern of negligence and showed that previous safety warnings at the plant had been shelved or ignored. Here was no "Act of God," as the insurance companies like to phrase it in the fine print of their contracts, but a shocking case of callousness on the part of a giant multinational corporation. Mother Teresa was on the next plane to Bhopal. At the airport, greeted by throngs of angry relatives of the victims, she was pressed to give her advice and counsel, and she did so unhesitatingly. I have a videotape of the moment. "Forgive," she said. "Forgive, forgive."

On the face of it, a strange injunction. How did she know there was anything to forgive? Had anybody asked for forgiveness? What are the duties of the poor to the rich in such a situation? And who is authorized to recommend, or to dispense, forgiveness?[5] In the absence of any answer to these questions, Mother Teresa's flying visit to Bhopal read like a hasty exercise in damage control, the expedient containment of righteous secular indignation.

Here is another film clip, this time of Mother Teresa at the airport in Madrid. She has flown in to lend her support to the clerical forces who are contesting the post-Franco legislation enabling divorce, abortion and birth control. The crowd at the terminal is composed of the highly traditional Spanish Right, with here and there a blue shirt, and a right arm flung skyward. This is one of the first political votes to decide whether or not Spain will evolve into a secular society. Mother Teresa has taken her stand in this debate, and she has taken it unequivocally on the conservative side—all the while claiming to remain above politics. Any exertion of this privilege is really an abuse, just as it was in Knock.

In London in 1988, Mother Teresa paid a visit ostensibly to discuss the growing problem of the

---

[5] If I may add a personal anecdote here: Mother Teresa was in the autumn of 1994 asked by the Calcutta newspapers to comment on *Hell's Angel*, the critical documentary which I and others had made on her work. She had not seen the documentary but her response was to say that she "forgave" us for making it. This was odd, since we had not sought forgiveness from her or from anyone else. Odder still if you have any inclination to ask by what right she assumes the power to forgive. There are even some conscientious Christians who would say that forgiveness, like the astringent of revenge, is reserved to a higher power.

city's homeless, who had forced the phrase "Cardboard City" into the language by dwelling in cardboard structures in parks and on the Embankment. Having spoken briefly on this topic, Mother Teresa was ushered into 10 Downing Street to meet in private with Prime Minister Margaret Thatcher. Mrs. Thatcher was famously unsentimental about the denizens of "Cardboard City" and indeed about most other forms of human failure and defeat, and it was not in any case the plight of the homeless that Mother Teresa wished to discuss. The two women went into conclave on the matter of abortion, which was then the subject of a private member's bill in the House of Commons, sponsored by the Liberal MP David Alton. Mr. Alton, who had sought to limit the availability of abortion, was in no doubt of the value of Mother Teresa's intervention. He told reporters that her meeting with Margaret Thatcher was an immense boost to his campaign, and he took credit for arranging the womanly summit. Whatever else may be said of this meeting, which occurred on the eve of a decisive parliamentary vote and was attended by a circus of cameras and scribes, the term "nonpolitical" does not apply to it very easily.

And now a photograph, or pair of photographs. Mother Teresa is seated in earnest conversation with Ronald Reagan and his chief of staff, Donald Regan. Both men wear expressions of the most determined sincerity. The photo opportunity occurs inside the White House in May 1985. Mother Teresa has been chosen to receive the Presidential Medal of Freedom. Her companions for the day are Frank Sinatra, James Stewart and Jeane Kirkpatrick, among other recipients. At the moment when the shutter falls on this shot, Ronald Reagan has every reason to be careful of Catholic susceptibility. His policy in Central America, which has resulted in his Cabinet officers defending the murders of four American nuns and the Archbishop of San Salvador, is deeply unpopular with the voters. One of his more daring lies—the claim that he had received a personal message from the Pope supporting his policy in the isthmus—has had to be retracted after causing considerable embarrassment. In the basement of the very building where Mother Teresa sits, a Marine Colonel named Oliver North (who forsook the Catholic Church for evangelical Pentecostalism after being vouchsafed a personal vision) is toiling away on an enterprise which will nearly succeed in destroying the Presidency that spawned it.

Stepping onto the portico of the White House, flanked by Ronald and Nancy, Mother Teresa knows just what to say:

I am most unworthy of this generous gift of our President, Mr. Reagan, and his wife and you people of the United States. But I accept it for the greater glory of God and in the name of the millions of poor people that this gift, in spirit and in love, will penetrate the hearts of the people.

This kind of modesty—speaking for God and for the poor—is now so standard on her part that nobody even notices it. Then:

I've never realized that you loved the people so tenderly. I had the experience, I was last time here, a sister from Ethiopia found me and said "Our people are dying. Our children are dying. Mother, do something." And the only person that came in my mind while she was talking, it was the President. And immediately I wrote to him, and I said, "I don't know, but this is what happened to me." And next day it was that immediately he arranged to bring food to our people.... Together, we are doing something beautiful for God.

Here was greater praise than Reagan could possibly have asked or hoped for. Not only was he told that he "loved the people so tenderly" but he was congratulated for his policy in Ethiopia. That policy, as it happened, was to support the claim of the Ethiopian ruling junta—the Dergue—to the supposed "territorial integrity" of the Ethiopian empire, which included (then) the insurgent people of Eritrea. General Mengistu Haile Mariam had deliberately used the weapon of starvation not just against Eritrea but also against domestic and regional dissent in other regions of the country. This had not prevented Mother Teresa from dancing attendance upon him and thereby shocking the human-rights community, which had sought to isolate his regime. That very isolation, however, had provided opportunities for "missionary work" to those few prepared to compromise. To invest such temporal and temporizing politics with the faint odor of sanctity, let alone with Mother Teresa's now-familiar suggestion of the operations of divine providence ("And next day it was...") is political in the extreme, but the White House press corps, deliberately ignorant of such considerations, duly gave the visit and the presentation its standard uncritical treatment.

During this same period, Mother Teresa visited Nicaragua and contrived to admonish the Sandinista revolutionary party. The Cardinal Archbishop of Managua, Miguel Obando y Bravo, was at that time the official patron and confessor of the *contras*, and was paid an admitted and regular stipend by the Central Intelligence Agency. Also at that time, the *contras* conceived it as their task to make a special target of clinics, schools, dairies and other "soft target" elements of the Nicaraguan system. And the *contras* believed—almost predictably—that they had on their side a miraculous Virgin who had appeared in the remote northern regions of the country. What they assuredly did have on their side was the most powerful state on earth, which openly announced that it would bring Nicaragua to heel by increasing the poverty and destitution of its wavering citizens. A consistent case might be made for following such a policy and for employing the Church in support of it, but however reasonable that case might be it could by no stretch of the imagination be described as a non-political one, or one animated by a love of the poor.

More lives were taken on purpose in the war on Nicaraguan "subversion" than have been saved by all the missionaries in Calcutta even by accident. Yet this brute utilitarian calculus is never employed against Mother Teresa, even by the sort of sophists who would deploy its moral and physical equivalent in her favor. So: silence on the death squads and on the Duvaliers and noisy complaint against the Sandinistas, and the whole act baptized as an apolitical intervention by someone whose kingdom is not of this world.

Visiting Guatemala during the same period, at a time when the killing fields were becoming too hideous even for the local oligarchy and its foreign patrons, and at a time when the planned extirpation of the Guatemalan Indians had finally become a global headline, Mother Teresa purred: "Everything was peaceful in the parts of the country we visited. I do not get involved in that sort of politics." At least, for once, she did not say that everything was "beautiful."

Afterword

We believe that taking that kind of position, Charlie, is not a Democrat or Republican issue. We think it's an issue of what's moral; it's about what's compassionate; it's the kind of values that Mother Teresa represents.

> Ralph Reed, chairman of Pat Robertson's
> "Christian Coalition," on *Charlie Rose*,
> 21 February 1995

.

DEAR ANN LANDERS:

Often the simple things in life can make the most difference. For example, when someone asked Mother Teresa how people without money or power can make the world a better place, she replied, "They should smile more."
—Prince George, B.C.

DEAR PRINCE:

What a splendid response. Thank you.

22 May 1995

Every day, the troubled and the despairing and the bewildered write their humble, nervous letters to the Ann Landers agony column. And every day, they are urged to seek counseling, to talk things over with their ministers, to pull their socks up, to play by the rules and look on the bright side. Most mornings, the jaunty column ends its brisk summary of the conventional wisdom with a "Gem of the Day," some fragment of cracker-barrel sapience or wry, *Reader's Digest*-style positive thinking. Recently, the above item was selected as the daily gem. Many Americans, schooled in the national dream of promise and abundance and opportunity, are condemned to experience life as a disappointment and to wonder if the fault is in themselves or in their stars that they are perpetual underlings. If this were not so, Ann Landers would be out of a job in the same way that so many of her readers are. But it is difficult to imagine many losers facing the day with a squarer jaw or a firmer, springier step as a consequence of imbibing this particular piece of counsel over their nutrition-free breakfast cereal. It is also doubtful whether a fortune-cookie maxim of such cretinous condescension would have been chosen even by Ann Landers unless it bore the imprimatur of Mother Teresa, one of the few untouchables in the mental universe of the mediocre and the credulous.

Intellectual snobbery? Only if the task of intellectuals is to urge Mr. and Mrs. Average to settle for little, or for less. Time and again, since I began the project of judging Mother Teresa's reputation by her actions and words rather than her actions and words by her reputation, I have been rebuked and admonished for ridiculing the household gods of the simple folk; for sneering at a woman who, to employ an old citation, "gives those in the gutter a glimpse of the stars." But is it not here that authentic intellectual snobbery exposes itself? We ourselves are far too sophisticated to believe in God and creationism and all that, say the more advanced defenders of the Teresa cult. But we *do* believe in religion—at least for other people. It is a means of marketing hope, and of instilling ethical precepts on the cheap. It is also a form of discipline. The followers of the late American guru Leo Strauss—a man who had a profound influence on the Republican Right wing—make this cynical point explicit in their otherwise arcane texts. There should be philosophy and knowledge for the elect, religion and sentimentality for the masses. By a bizarre coincidence of political opportunism, these Straussian forces are today ranged in alliance with the Christian fundamentalist cohort, founded by Pat Robertson but represented in public by the more cosmetic Ralph Reed. As can be seen from the excerpt above, Mr. Reed knows how to use a script when he is in a tight corner. Challenged on his prospectus for a

"Christian America" that cares for people before they are born and after they are dead but is only interested in clerical coercion for the years in between, Mr. Reed immediately reaches for the Gorgon's head of Mother Teresa and turns his questioners into stone. This would be even funnier if the Christian Coalition did not have its roots in the most vulgar strain of anti-Catholicism, but as Mother Teresa has shown in her moments with John-Roger and Michèle Duvalier, and as her Church has shown in its alliance with mullahs and ayatollahs, there exists a sort of reverse ecumenicism which unites all versions of the "faithful" against any version of the dreaded "secular humanist" Enlightenment.

Agnes Bojaxhiu knows perfectly well that she is conscripted by people like Ralph Reed, that she is a fund-raising icon for clerical nationalists in the Balkans, that she has furnished PR-type cover for all manner of cultists and shady businessmen (who are often the same thing), that her face is on vast highway billboards urging the state to take on the responsibility of safeguarding the womb. By no word or gesture has she ever repudiated any of these connections or alliances. Nor has she ever deigned to respond to questions about her friendship with despots. She merely desires to be taken at her own valuation and to be addressed universally as "Mother Teresa." Her success is not, therefore, a triumph of humility and simplicity. It is another chapter in a millennial story which stretches back to the superstitious childhood of our species, and which depends on the exploitation of the simple and the humble by the cunning and the single-minded.

As Edward Gibbon observed about the modes of worship prevalent in the Roman world, they were "considered by the people as equally true, by the philosopher as equally false and by the magistrate as equally useful." Mother Teresa descends from each element in this grisly triptych. She has herself purposely blurred the supposed distinction between the sacred and the profane, to say nothing of the line that separates the sublime from the ridiculous. It is past time that she was subjected to the rational critique that she has evaded so arrogantly and for so long.